GRASMERE

A HISTORY
IN 55½ BUILDINGS

Grasmere

A History in 55½ Buildings

Grasmere History Group

Grasmere: A History in Fifty-Five and a Half Buildings
First Published in 2019.

© Grasmere History Group, 2019

Thank you to all who have offered the use of photographs and other archival materials.

ISBN: 978-1-9163207-0-3 (PRINT)

Contents

Foreword

This book was written collaboratively by members of Grasmere History Group, a local history group that has been meeting once a month since 2012 at the Wordsworth Trust. The group is open to anyone with an interest in Grasmere's history.

In the book we offer a snapshot of the history of Grasmere as told through a selection of its buildings. We chose the buildings included not for their importance, but to give a sense of the social history of the village over time. Some of the buildings have their foundations in the Middle Ages; some were constructed in the last decade. You will find recurring characters and families – from prolific Victorian builder Levi Hodgson to the Green family, who at one time owned much of the village – famous residents and famous visitors.

Although the title promises a history in 55½ buildings, there are only 54 entries. This can be explained through the building histories themselves. Some of our buildings used to be one building and became several; some used to be several and became one. In a couple of cases, one entry covers an estate rather than a single building. The 'half' building is the Easedale Tarn Refreshment Hut, which in its heyday was half-boulder, half-building, and is now barely a footprint.

The book combines new findings with research from exhibitions the group have held at the Wordsworth Trust's community gallery, including on Grasmere during the First World War, Grasmere House History, and the growth of tourism in the Lake District.

The group benefits greatly from access to the Wordsworth Trust archives, and is grateful for permission to use the many wonderful historical images included, as well as those from private collections.

The introduction gives an overview of Grasmere's wider history, and provides context for many of the particular building histories.

We have aimed to be as accurate as we can but there is always more to say and more to uncover. We hope this book might be the start of many more conversations.

Some of the buildings included are open to the public, but many are private homes. We ask that you respect the privacy of the residents, landowners and homeowners.

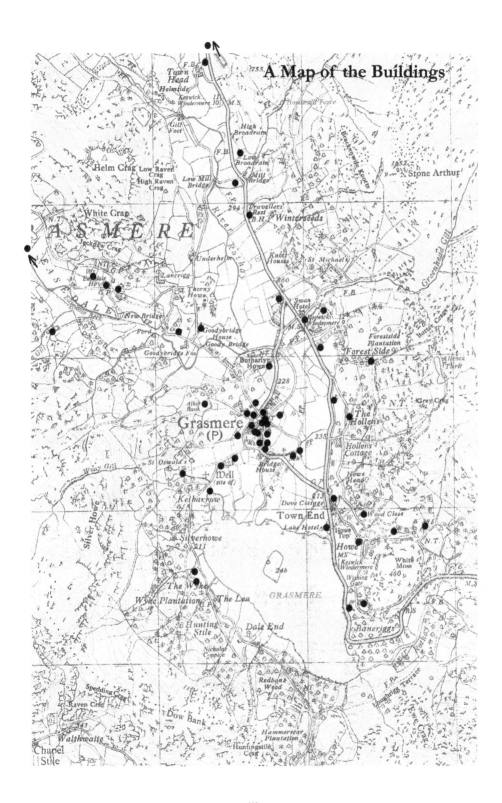

A Map of the Buildings

Introduction

Grasmere village is situated in the centre of the Lake District National Park in the County of Cumbria, in the north west of England. The area was granted UNESCO World Heritage status in 2017 in the cultural landscape category and Grasmere featured in the submission.

This book gives a version of the history of Grasmere as seen through a selection of its buildings, the people who built them, worked in them and lived in them. This introduction covers the early history of Grasmere and the surrounding area, the peoples who have lived here and its development over the centuries to the present day. It includes social aspects as well as key historical moments and changes. It traces the establishment and expansion of the village and community as different trades, industries and livelihoods flourished and allowed the village itself to thrive and grow.

The historic buildings of Grasmere have a quality and homogeneity, with good examples of both common and rare Lakeland vernacular architecture, historic shop fronts and larger gentry houses and hotels including thirty-nine listed buildings. The palette of building materials reflects the underlying geology of dark grey and purple slate stone, with contrasting blue grey detailing for quoins,

Thomas Colman Dibdin, 'Grasmere, Westmorland' (1845)

1

window and door surrounds, drip moulds and chimneys.

The village of Grasmere takes its name from the adjacent lake, 'the lake flanked by grass', a mere being a word for a shallow lake.

Early Grasmere: settlement and conflict

People have probably lived in and around Grasmere for several millennia. The end of Arctic conditions of the Ice Age had encouraged growth of vegetation, and gradually forests covered all but the highest peaks. The flat valley bottoms were swampy and covered in dense vegetation.

Early evidence of habitation nearby can be seen in the Neolithic Castlerigg stone circle eleven miles to the north of Grasmere, near Keswick, and the Neolithic axe factory four miles away at Great Langdale. There is an Iron Age hillfort on Carrock Fell, and a hillfort eight miles away at Shoulthwaite, Thirlmere, which was thought to be Iron Age, although evidence shows its last construction was in the seventh century AD. Around 80AD the Romans built a fort called Galava, with a turf wall and timber buildings, in what is now Ambleside. A stone version was built around the year 130AD on the instructions of Emperor Hadrian. From Ambleside there are Roman roads to both Ravenglass via Wrynose pass and Brougham via High Street. When the Romans arrived, Celts were occupying settlements on the coast and along rivers. The Romans withdrew from Britain in 410AD so their influence lasted over 300 years. At the end of this period the inhabitants of Cumberland could be described as Cumbric-speaking native Romano-Britons.

In the fifth and sixth centuries England was colonised by Angles and Saxons who liked fertile valleys for pasture. The Romano-Britons survived in the remoter valleys and high moorlands. Cumberland formed the core of the British kingdom of Rheged. For the rest of the first millennium, Cumbria was contested by several peoples who warred over the area, including the Brythonic kingdom of Strathclyde and the Anglian kingdom of Northumbria.

Danish Vikings burnt down Carlisle in 875AD. Norse Vikings invaded and settled in the tenth century, migrating from Ireland and the Isle of Man. They brought their Herdwick sheep and penetrated deep into Lakeland, clearing forest and scrub from the valleys. Old Norse speech was used till the thirteenth century and even now forms a significant part of Cumbrian dialect. Old Norse names survive today in Grasmere in the River Rothay (the 'trout river') and Helm crag ('helmet crag').

Duvenald (Dunmail), the British king of Strathclyde, was attacked by the combined forces of King Edmund of Northumbria and Malcolm King of Scots and retreated into the heart of the Lake District. In 945AD Dunmail met the kings in battle at the pass that divides Grasmere from Thirlmere and was defeated. Cumbria was then handed over to Malcolm on the understanding that he lent his support to the English King whenever required. The pile of stones at the top of raise is said to commemorate the battle, and the pass bears Dunmail's name.

Grasmere in the Middle Ages

At the time of the Norman conquest of England in 1066 Grasmere was still part of Scotland and thus was excluded from the Domesday Book survey of 1086. The Normans conquered the area in 1092 and created the baronies of Kentdale and Westmorland.

The area to the south of Grasmere was under ecclesiastical control for many centuries. Furness Abbey was founded in 1123. The monks of the abbey were large landowners and the most powerful body in what was then a remote border territory. Though they owned small parcels of land north of Grasmere their main lands were to the south and did not include Grasmere.

Grasmere's first church was named after Oswald, King of Northumbria, who died in 642AD. The earliest record of a church is believed to date to the William de Lyndseye rent roll of 1203. The first recorded clerk or priest was Henry de Galdington from 1254. The present church, still called St Oswald's, dates from 1250 and stands on or near the site of the original church. It was referred to as a chapel, as the mother church was in Kendal.

The establishment of the church indicates a settled community in Grasmere in need of a permanent place to worship. Grasmere Manor was part of the Manor of Windermere in the Kentdale Barony, the first grant of which was given to Ivo de Talebois by William the Conqueror. The Kentdale Barony was amalgamated into the county of Westmorland in 1226. It is recorded that in 1247:

'The King (Henry III) has assigned to Agnes who was the wife of William de Lancastre in dower the manors of Geirstang, Estan, Scotford, Stothagh and Kerneford, in co. Lancaster, and Grasmere, Langdon, Crosthwayt and Le Lyth with the appurtenances in co. Westmerland.'

Historical evidence from the twelfth century onwards indicates that the physical geography and climate of the Lake District enabled widespread sheep farming and the export of wool. By the fourteenth century there was a thriving market in the townships of Kendal and Ambleside for ready-woven cloth for export to other parts of England and abroad. To serve this industry a series of fulling mills had been constructed in Grasmere along the banks of the River Rothay and at Easedale. Fulling was a step in woollen clothmaking which involved the cleansing of cloth to eliminate oils, dirt, and other impurities, and to make it thicker. The fulling mills have been described as a revolutionary development changing the pattern of the agricultural economy, not only by speedier processing of larger quantities of a more weather-proof cloth, but also by introducing urban manufacturing and economic concepts into the rural manors and monastic estates.

The earliest fulling mill referred to in the surviving documentation may be the manorial fulling mill of Grasmere belonging to William de Lyndseye, perhaps serving the areas of Grasmere, Langdale and Loughrigg, situated at the manorial centre. The wool industry and trade at that time were controlled by landowners, and dues extracted from the transportation of cloth.

In 1283 when William de Lyndseye died his property included a forest, a fishery, a fulling mill, a brew-house and a chapel. At that time there were sixteen tenants who were named but the location of the properties within the village is not known. The manor was later held successively by the de Couplands, de Courcys and Margaret, Countess of Richmond. In 1285 the village fair was held in the churchyard. Grasmere seems to have been a thriving community.

In 1332 a list of tenants included three with names implying where they lived in Grasmere: John de la Wra (The Wray), Thomas de Asedale (Easedale) and William de Ayesdale (Easedale).

By 1390 there were thirty-eight houses in Grasmere.

Wool products travelled to and from Grasmere along the packhorse tracks which linked Grasmere to the main centres of medieval trade and commerce at Ambleside and Keswick. In 1494 Grasmere is recorded as having ten fulling mills.

Alongside the wool and cloth industries, Grasmere had a growing woodland economy. Woodland provided food, fuel and building materials and by the medieval period such value that it was actively protected and came under the direct control of the lord of the manor. In Ambleside, Grasmere and Langdale, tenants were required to pay 'greenhew' for the right to cut the green parts of trees in the woods and forests for fodder for animals. Tenants had the right to graze their animals on the common land and Commoners still exist in Grasmere today with grazing rights. Coppicing and charcoal burning would have been carried out. Locations of three bloomeries – charcoal-fuelled iron-smelting furnaces – have been identified: one at Far Easedale and two near Dunmail Raise. Two kilnwood kilns (used to dry timber), and ten potash kilns (which burnt bracken to create the fertiliser potash), have been identified in the Grasmere valley. It seems that some fullers may have worked several kilns, although not at the same time. This would have permitted bracken to regenerate in one area whilst another was being cut over. There is a lime kiln in a wall between Lancrigg wood (How Coppice) and Stubdale.

Following the dissolution of the monasteries in 1537 Grasmere became a Civil Parish. The village continued to thrive and grow, though slowly.

Industrial Changes

In 1574 there were forty-nine houses.

The first map to show Gresmere (sic) is by Christopher Saxton in 1576; it shows the church, the lake, a bridge over the river and Dunbalrase (sic) Stones to the north.

In 1577 the plague appeared in Grasmere and the first outbreak lasted over a year. A second came in 1597/8. The ill-kept registers of Grasmere make it impossible to say how many lives were lost, but in November 1578 there were twelve burials, and ten the following January.

In the sixteenth century Grasmere had three folds used as pinfolds. Two were for stock straying from manors of Wythburn (to the north) and Rydal (to the south), and one for strays belonging to the tenants of Grasmere. The site of one can still be seen near White Bridge. These indicate the importance of livestock to villagers.

Farms are built or more likely rebuilt from the end of the 16th century: Blintarngill (1572) and Brimahead (1574, now Brimmer Head), Underhelm (1576), Syke Side (1586), High Scorecrag (1601), How Head (1612, now just the barn remains), Low Broadrain (1630, now Broadrayn), Knot House (1638), Hollens (1644), Padmire/Pavement End (1644), Goody Bridge, Town Head, How Top, Low Fold and High Easedale. Brimmer Head, Underhelm, Knot House and Town Head are still in use today.

In 1674 there were sixty-two dwellings shown in the Hearth Tax records.

The late sixteenth and seventeenth centuries were a period of decline for the wool and cloth trade in the Lake District, and different industries emerged. Slate quarrying was carried out at White Moss by the late seventeenth century, expanded in the nineteenth century and closed in the twentieth century. There were also two quarries in Easedale, one called James's, the other at Jackdaw Crag.

The Greenhead Gill mine complex is one of the early lead working sites in Cumbria. It has two separate processing areas about 140m apart on the east side of Greenhead Gill. The documentary and archaeological evidence points to at least two separate phases of exploitation at the mines on Greenhead Gill. The first, around

1600, was one of several trial workings established around Grasmere. In the late nineteenth century the original workings were revived and exploratory working was undertaken to the south of the main complex using drilling and powder-blasting technology.

In 1672 there were several smithys in Grasmere: one at How Head above Town End run by George Otley, another run by

Smithy at White Bridge

William Mackereth, though the whereabouts are uncertain, and a more ancient one at Winterseeds run by John Watson. After the turnpike road was created in 1770 in the bottom of the valley, this position – accessible only up a steep rise – became inconvenient for custom so another smithy was opened below, where William Simpson worked.

Grasmere's famous Rushbearing Ceremony is centred on St. Oswald's Church. The earliest mention of a rush custom at Grasmere is a payment of one shilling in 1680, 'for ale bestowed on those who brought rushes and repaired the church'. The ceremony has ancient origins. Originally the floors of churches were simply composed of compacted earth, which was strewn with rushes. Once a year rushes would be cut and carried to the church to cover the earth floor. The floor has been paved at Grasmere since 1840 but

Rushbearing in 1947

the tradition continues to be upheld. The Ceremony is still held annually and features a colourful procession through the village streets with bearings made from rushes and flowers. In this procession are six Maids of Honour, dressed in matching green costumes, carrying a white sheet holding the strewing rushes. A brass band and the church choir also contribute, and all who wish to join in by carrying their own decorated rushbearing.

The first village school was built from an endowment in 1685 and is now the Grasmere Gingerbread shop. Previously, children were taught by the curate in the church. The Tithe barn, which is attached to the Rectory, was built in 1687 and became the Parish Hall.

There were plentiful inns in Grasmere which point to not just local custom, but the importance of Grasmere as a resting place for travellers. On Red Bank there was Nichols (near Huntingstile) and Keldbergh (1375, now the site of Kellbarrow). In Easedale, an inn at Jackdaw Cottage. In Town End, the Dove and Olive Bough (now Dove Cottage), and on the way to Keswick, The White Swan Inn (1650, now the Swan Hotel) and the Travellers Rest (1668). In the centre of the village, there was an inn at Church Stile (1638).

1700-1800: roadbuilding and estate-making

The Grasmere Manor had been granted by Charles II to his wife Queen Catherine. After her death in 1705 it was granted to the Lowther family, Earls of Lonsdale, under a lease from the Crown. This marked the beginning of a shift in land ownership. By the late nineteenth century there were a number of principal landowners, including the Le Fleming family of Rydal.

Grasmere consisted of several hamlets: Church Town, Town End, Town Head and later around The Swan Inn and Boothwaite/Easedale. Bridges over the rivers were key assets and needed constant maintenance. In 1712 the chief constable was ordered to contract to repair White Bridge, and in 1714, the bridge was again presented as being very dangerous. In 1727 a contract was made

'to pull down all and every part of the common and county

bridge called and known by the name of Stock Bridge near Grasmere Townend at the entrance into Grasmere Field, a great part thereof is now fallen down and the remainder being in great decay and very dangerous, and to build a new firm stone bridge in the same place.'

Widening of Church Bridge, 1926-27

In 1730 Church Bridge was replaced. The Willie Goodwaller Bridge on the packhorse route at Far Easedale is Grade II listed and so is Church Bridge.

In 1724 Daniel Defoe, an early tourist to the Lakes, described the area as 'the wildest, most barren and frightful of any that I have passed over in England'. There were no roads for wheeled traffic in these valleys till after 1750; all transport of goods was done by packhorses or men along paths which kept as much as possible to the hillsides. This was necessary because of the marshy ground in the valley bottom.

The approach to Grasmere from Ambleside was by the pack-horse way which still runs behind Rydal Mount past Brockstones, over White Moss, to How Top and down to Town End. This is known as the coffin route because the corpses of people from Rydal were brought for burial in Grasmere along it. Two large flat stones, referred to as 'coffin stones', where the pallbearers could place the coffin so they could rest during the journey, are still in position on the route. The packhorse way from Langdale over Hunting Stile was used for bringing the corpses of Langdale people for burial in Grasmere, which continued until 1845. The corpses were brought to Grasmere church because it was the Parish church of the Ecclesiastical Parish of Grasmere that alone held burial rights. The area included Ambleside Above Stock (beck), Langdale, Loughrigg and Rydal. The Keswick Road passed up the hill by Turn How and it can still be traced winding in and out among the grassy hummocks to the top of Dunmail Raise. Further tracks went up Far Easedale to Borrowdale, alongside Tongue Ghyll to Patterdale and several routes to the Langdale valley.

In 1768 both Dunmail Raise and Smithy Bridges were in great decay and 'ought to be repaired at the public expense of the County' and the same for White Bridge in 1776 and again both Church and Stock Bridges in 1790.

The poet Thomas Gray, who visited in 1769, said of Grasmere: 'Not a single red tile, no Gentleman's flaring house, or garden walls, break in upon the repose of this little unsuspected paradise; but all is peace, rusticity, and happy poverty, in its neatest, most becoming attire.'
Something of the 'rusticity and happy poverty' that Gray celebrates can be found in the tangle of cottages, yards and lanes to the rear of Red Lion Square.

The Turnpike road from Ambleside to Keswick was opened in 1770. As you leave Grasmere and start to climb Dunmail Raise look to the left and you will see Toll Bar Cottage, a reminder of the direct tax that was levied on all road users. To the south the route was on the old road from Town End to White Moss, then via Rydal, Ambleside and Windermere to Kendal. The Red Lion Inn (1769) was built to meet the demand of additional travellers.

In 1770 the Jefferys map shows roads and names twenty houses which can still be identified today.

In 1777 the Window Tax records show fifty-one dwellings.

In 1778 Father Thomas West published the first tourist guide *A Guide to the Lakes* in which he recommended the best spots for visitors to stand and admire the landscape. Before long, the writings of poets such as Wordsworth, Southey and Coleridge were promoting the beauty and splendour of the landscape to a nation eager to escape the growing cities.

A poster publicising the fair to be held in 1790 reads:
Grassmere, July 30, 1790.
Notice is hereby given, That there will annually be exposed to sale by private contract, At Grassmere, in the county of Westmorland, A quantity of sheep of different sorts, also horses and horned cattle of different sorts, yarn and wool.

The sale will be on every first Tuesday in September annually, and commence on Tuesday 7th Day of September next ensuing the date hereof. Where it is expected the shew will be pretty numerous both of sheep then fit for present use and for grassing, as the neighbouring shepherds have agreed thereto, and will endeavour to promote and encourage the same.

Kendal: Printed by James Ashburner.

1800 onwards: Romantics and Tourists

From 1801 large houses had started to appear in Grasmere with The Wyke, typically built for Lancashire businessmen seeking a country escape. Allan Bank was built in 1805 in parkland to the west of Grasmere village.

William Wordsworth and his sister Dorothy arrived in Grasmere in 1799 and moved into what is now called Dove Cottage. He described Grasmere as 'the loveliest spot that man hath ever found'. Dorothy wrote her famous journal describing Grasmere and the countryside 1800-1803. In 1808 they moved to Allan Bank, then to the Rectory before moving to Rydal Mount in 1813. From 1809 to 1820 Thomas De Quincey lived in Dove Cottage.

Famous artists were inspired by the area. J.M.W. Turner visited the Lakes in 1797, 1801 and 1831. Ignoring the Picturesque guidebooks, his paintings (worked up in the studio during the Winter from sketches done at the time) took some liberties with the topography, but are reckoned to capture the elemental forces of the Lakes more than any other works. He made several sketches and paintings of Grasmere which are held by Tate Britain.

In 1811 there were sixty-two dwellings. In 1828 the map by Thomas Hodgson marks thirty houses by name.

In 1822 William Wordsworth published his own guide book, *A Description of the Scenery of the Lakes in the North of England*, which sold rapidly and encouraged many more visitors. The ongoing effects of the French Revolution and the Napoleonic Wars meant that wealthy tourists, who might otherwise have done a grand tour of Europe, were forced to travel closer to home. Over the years many royal visitors and heads of states have visited Grasmere.

In 1824 the route over White Moss was described as 'very dangerous and incommodious to travellers by reason of the steepness and narrowness thereof'. The lower route via Penny Rock was created and opened in the late 1820s. Penny Rock was said to be so named because a penny was added on to the rates or to the toll fee to cover the cost of blasting through the rock.

In 1829, a commercial directory records that Grasmere was by now a township with 'several gentleman's seats, many of which are richly decked with sylvan ornaments and command splendid views of the amphitheatre of mountains which surround the lake'. The directory gives a list of the householders of the village, some with their occupations. The occupations included: Rector, schoolmaster, innkeeper, corn miller, stonemason, perpetual overseer (collector of taxes and rents), shoemaker, blacksmith, toll collector, victualler, joiner, actuary and one person who was both tailor and grocer. In addition, there were twenty-four farmers in 1829, including two women. Twelve of the farmers were Yeomen, including one woman. Records show an annual Sheep Fair was held in Grasmere in the same year.

Some land in the area had been enclosed from the fourteenth century onwards. Strips were fenced off from the common field. During the eighteenth and nineteenth centuries, enclosures were by means of local acts of Parliament, called the Inclosure Acts. These parliamentary enclosures consolidated strips in the open fields into more cohesive units, and enclosed much of the remaining pasture commons or wastes. Parliamentary enclosures usually provided commoners with some other land in compensation for the loss of common rights, although often of poor quality and limited extent. Enclosure consisted of exchange in land, and an extinguishing of common rights. This allowed farmers to consolidate and fence off plots of land, in contrast to multiple small strips spread out and separated.

There is a list and map showing the field names and the owners for Grasmere in 1847. The field names reflect the usage or state of the land, for example: 'Tenters', which were wooden frames for drying the woollen cloth to prevent shrinkage, and 'Mire' describing wet ground. Commoners have the right to graze livestock on common land and these rights still apply today to Commoners of Grasmere on White Moss.

The Penny Black postage stamp was introduced in 1840 and enabled the Postal Service to offer a standard delivery price across the country. The first Post Office in Grasmere opened sometime between 1835 and 1859 at Tanner Croft. The two original Tanner Croft houses were built in 1835 and the Post Office would have been in what is now called number two. It moved to the adjoining larger purpose-built property when that was built in the 1860s (now number one).

The national census of 1841 recorded people's names, their occupations and the name of their house. There were 79 dwellings and 332 people. The tourist industry was given a further major boost when the railway reached Windermere in 1847, placing Grasmere within reach of the cities of northern England, some of whose industrialists built large houses on the fringes of the village.

The horse drawn Royal Mail service between Windermere and Keswick, operated by Rigg's of Windermere, whose business started in 1847, passed through Grasmere. The regular coach services that now passed along this route stimulated the growth of Grasmere as a place of coaching inns where travellers could spend the night, and horses could be changed, refreshed and shod. The

Red Lion Hotel was a coaching inn, and some of the outbuildings that cluster up against this building were probably used as stables and blacksmith's forges. At one time, the Rothay Hotel (now Wordsworth Hotel) stabled 125 horses.

When Wordsworth died in 1850 and was buried in St. Oswald's churchyard, Grasmere was reinforced as a centre of literary tourism. Visitors flocked to the village to have their photographs taken in front of the Wordsworth family and Hartley Coleridge's graves.

Grasmere Sports in 1876, photograph by William Baldry.

The Grasmere Sports were first held in the 1840s following the Sheep Fair. It soon became a popular annual event, also drawing in vast numbers of visitors. The first Guides Race to the top of Silver How was held in 1868 but now the course over Butter Crags is much shorter. Since 1868 the Sports have been a regular annual event, unbroken except for the two periods of the First and Second World Wars. The main sports attractions have always been The Guide's Race, Cumberland and Westmorland style Wrestling, and the Hound Trails, all of which have prize money.

Grasmere's picturesque qualities and the Wordsworth legacy also led to the construction of several large purpose-built hotels. Brown's Hotel was built at Town End in 1855 (later renamed The Prince of Wales and now The Daffodil). The Cascade Hotel was built at White Moss during this period and demolished in the early twentieth-century by the Friends of the Lake District. Some large houses were converted into hotels: Moss Head built in 1630 became the Rothay Hotel (now the Wordsworth Hotel). Hollins became The

Hollins & Lowther Hotel shortly before 1851. Later, Dale Cottage became Dale Lodge Hotel in 1905.

The National School was built on the current site in 1854 (infant school built 1862) and enlarged in 1879; now Grasmere Primary School. Free education started in 1893 and prior to this had to be paid for. A plaque on the side records its early history.

In 1855 the turnpike records show that 15,420 vehicles journeyed beyond Ambleside to Grasmere and Keswick. The Toll gates were removed in 1875 by Government statute.

The Crimean War (1853-6) had revealed just how stretched Britain's military resources could be in the event of a conflict. Then the tension which arose between Britain and France in 1858 led the Secretary of State for War to issue a letter in May 1859 to Lords Lieutenant of counties authorising them to raise Rifle Volunteer Corps. The 6th Westmorland (Grasmere) RVC, with a sub-division in Langdale was commissioned on the 17th April 1860, with forty-nine men under the command of Captain Jasper Selwyn (plus twenty-six men in Langdale).

The two rifle ranges of 300 and 800 yards located on Silver How near Wyke Plantation date from 1860. Remains of the Range Officer's hut can still be seen. The Drill Hall was part of Red Lion property and located on the opposite side of the road to the Inn.

The first Ordnance Survey map was surveyed in 1859 showing the minute detail to which we are accustomed today: houses, hotels, barns, a corn mill, roads, tracks, footpaths, rivers, streams, as well as sheepfolds and field walls.

In 1871 the number of dwellings had risen to 177 and the population to 796.

Both the influx of tourists and the growing population presented growing needs. Working Men's Reading Rooms were erected 1873. A Wesleyan Chapel was built 1874. It closed for services in 2008 and is now a bistro.

In 1881 the Rifle Volunteer Corps (RVCs) were constituted as volunteer regiments of the Border Regiment and Grasmere RVC became part of the 2nd (Westmorland) Volunteer Battalion. In 1908 the volunteer battalions were merged with the militia and the yeomanry to form the territorial force and it is likely that H Company of the (Cumberland & Westmorland) Battalion of the Border Regiment continued to use the ranges.

Grasmere Rifle Club, 1912, photograph by T. Wilson Jnr.

The Thirlmere aqueduct was constructed between 1886 and 1894 to carry water to Manchester. The navvies who did the tunnelling were housed in huts on White Moss (the Encampment) and Dunmail Raise. The 1891 census recorded a spike in the population of Grasmere to 1017 due to the number of navvies and their families. The construction manager's house was moved to the current position of Dunnabeck.

The first doctor to live and run a surgery in Grasmere was Dr. Ben Johnston from about 1886 until he died in 1946.

The Wordsworth Trust was founded (as the Dove Cottage Trust) in December 1890. Its creation followed a successful appeal for funds to purchase Dove Cottage, 'for the eternal possession of those who love English poetry all over the world'. Dove Cottage itself opened to visitors on July 27th 1891. The museum was moved from Old Sykeside (originally Sykeside farm) to the present barn in 1979. The archives hold original manuscripts, books, paintings and much more. The Trust organises talks, literary events and exhibitions and continues research into the Lake poets and their work.

Grasmere amateur dramatic society was performing dialect plays in 1893. They were revived in 1923-37, mostly written by Mrs. Eleanor Rawnsley. The Grasmere Players society goes back to 1949 and they continue to perform in the Village Hall. Canon Hardwicke Drummond Rawnsley, became a co-founder of the National Trust in 1895 following a failed effort to secure Grasmere island for the nation. He was the vicar of Low Wray church from 1878. He lived at Allan Bank in Grasmere from 1915. He bequeathed the house to the National Trust, which prior to that had only held land, and not houses. Although he died in 1920, his second wife Eleanor continued to live at Allan Bank until her death in 1959. The National Trust today own a lot of land and many farms and houses in Grasmere.

In the 1901 census, the number of dwellings was 199 and the population 782.

Grasmere New Hall opened in 1903 and is still in use as the village hall. The Lake Artists Society, founded in 1904, holds its annual exhibition in the hall.

With the outbreak of the First World War in 1914, territorial units were given the option of serving overseas and many volunteered to do so. 122 people from Grasmere enrolled in the armed forces. Twenty-five died during the war. Their names are on a memorial plaque in the church.

In 1916, with the British Army heavily committed across the channel, the Government decided that a home defence force was required once more and action was taken to encourage the establishment of Voluntary Training Corps. These comprised the young, the middle-aged and those exempt from military service. In 1917 the Westmorland Corps was recognised by the War Office, including a detachment in Grasmere.

William Peascod with bearing, 1912 (died 1917)

Grasmere Citizens Association was formed in 1919 and ended in 1960.

Horse drawn coaches thrived well into the 20th century when cars and buses eventually superseded them, though Brown's of Ambleside ran horse drawn char-a-bancs right up to 1939. Motor bus companies were operating in the Lakeland shortly after the turn of the century but the main impetus came after the 1914-19 war and in the 1920s, when not only did established companies expand, but one-man bus firms started on all sides, usually run by ex-servicemen. The Lake District Road Traffic Company started a Bowness to Grasmere service in 1904 and by 1920 its big Yellow Peril buses were a familiar feature of Lakeland roads.

In 1931 county records give a population of 988.

In 1932 one of the first Youth Hostels in the country opened at Thorney Howe, Easedale. Since 2011 it has been an independent hostel.

With the outbreak of the Second World War in 1939, the government, again, saw the need for a home defence force, this time in the form of the Home Guard or 'Dad's Army' as it became known. The County Archives in Kendal have papers showing that the Grasmere Platoon of C Company of the 9th Westmorland (Lakes) Battalion of the Home Guard used the Silver How range during this time — with some grumbling because of the climb involved! Two soldiers from Grasmere died in World War Two. Their names are on the memorial plaque in the church.

There is a concrete pill box on the west side of the road leaving Grasmere to the north which is a legacy of World War Two. Originally it would have housed guns and would have been used in the event of an enemy invasion to control the transport network of the valleys.

During the war evacuees from Newcastle upon Tyne, which was heavily bombed, were allocated to live with local families and attended the school.

The twentieth century has seen further development with a very high proportion of the buildings in the centre now converted to use as shops, catering outlets or as hotels, guest houses or self-catering accommodation.

Butharlyp Howe was a private house built in 1865 and became YHA Grasmere Butharlyp Howe Youth Hostel in 1958. It still operates today.

Many administrative organisational changes have been made since it was made an Urban District Council in 1894. Now Grasmere is part of the Lakes Parish in the county of Cumbria.

St. Oswald's Women's Fellowship was formed in 1960 and later became the Grasmere Fellowship. Grasmere Village Society (GVS) was formed in 1977 in order to protect the site of the Rothay Hotel. The society purchased the hotel by public subscription, then restored and opened it as the Wordsworth Hotel in 1981. It is still owned by the GVS who lease it to hoteliers to run the hotel.

The Rothay Trust, appointed by the GVS, built and now maintain the permissive path along the riverside from Broadgate car park to the Gingerbread shop. This can also be reached from the car and coach park in Stock Lane by crossing the Millennium Bridge, which was also built by GVS, and maintained by the Rothay Trust.

In 1984 Grasmere Conservation Area was designated by the Lake District National Park Authority and later amended in 2008. There is a separate Conservation Area around Town End. Conservation areas are legally defined as areas of 'special architectural or historic interest, the character or appearance of which it is desirable to preserve or enhance'. The special character relates to the quality and interest of an area as a whole rather than just individual buildings. Historic England have listed thirty-nine buildings in Grasmere, including the War Memorial and the AA box at the top of Dunmail Raise.

Grasmere in the Twenty-first Century

The number of dwellings continues to increase with more houses added in 2013 at Broadgate Orchard and in 2018 at Greenhead Fold near The Swan Hotel.

In 2018 the Rectory and Tithe Barn were sold by the Diocese and became private property.

In 2020 the Wordsworth Trust will open a new learning space, an improved museum and a community sensory garden as part of a National Lottery Heritage Fund refurbishment scheme.

Grasmere continues to change and grow according to need and social shifts. Some social groups currently active in Grasmere include: a local branch of the Women's Institute, Book Group, the Royal Antediluvian Order of Buffaloes (the Buffs), glee club, Knit & Nat, Fellowship, church choir, and of course, the History Group that wrote this book.

In recent decades the demographics of the village have changed, partly because of the high percentage of dwellings that are holiday homes or rentals, estimated to be at least 42%. This has resulted in the low number of residents in 2019. There are fewer young people under the age of eighteen, estimated at sixty-five, and the local football team stopped playing in 2005. The number of retired people has increased. These changes are reflected in the average household size of residents which has reduced to about 2.2 people from 3.9 people ninety years earlier and an average of about five in the nineteenth century.

Fortunately, much has been written about Grasmere over the centuries in official records, and specialist books covering various aspects of life in the Lake District. Three people who lived locally deserve recognition for their work in recording histories of Grasmere. Firstly, Mary Louisa Armitt who lived in Hawkshead and Rydal. Secondly, Gertrude Simpson, who spent all her adult life in Grasmere, was an authority on the folklore, old traditions and customs of the area, and made a study of the origin of place names and of the dialect. Thirdly, Gertrude's sister Eleanor 'Nellie' Foster Simpson, who was an author and secretary to Canon Hardwicke Rawnsley, later becoming his second wife. She kept a diary of local life which has survived.

In 300 years Grasmere has gone from being a remote and rural farming parish in a little-known part of upland England to being one of the best-known villages in the Lake District, in which tourism and commerce now dominate. Many of the original houses have disappeared, some have been demolished and some have been replaced. Some of the larger houses have been divided into multiple dwellings, many in the second half of the twentieth century.

The story of Grasmere is told here through the buildings which can be seen today. Each of the buildings is described through a combination of their history, the people who lived in them and events from the sixteenth century to the present day.

— Stewart Sutcliffe

Table showing changes in the total number of dwellings and the resident population over 700 years.

Year	1283	1390	1574	1674	1777	1811	1841	1871	1901	1931	2019
Dwellings	16	38	49	62	51	62	79	177	199	251	550
Population	68	167	209	239	218	265	332	796	782	988	700

References
(pre-1811 population estimated based on 1811's people per dwelling ratio)
1293, 1390, 1574: Barony of Kentdale records
1674: Hearth Tax records
1777: Window Tax records
1811: local records
1841, 1871, 1901: National censuses
1931: County Report; the number of dwellings is estimated from the number of people per dwelling in 1901
2019: Local survey of dwellings by the Grasmere First Responders; an estimate for the resident population from the 2011 census, the Electoral Register and other sources

1. Raise Cottage   4. The Old Mill
2. Toll Bar Cottage   5. The Traveller's Rest
3. Broadrayne

1. Raise Cottage

Raise Cottage was built on land owned by the Green family in the late nineteenth century. The Manchester Corporation rented the cottage from the Greens for workers during the transformation of Thirlmere into a reservoir. In 1888, the tenant was an engine driver working on the Manchester waterworks. From 1893 Manchester Corporation's tenancy was sub-let to the local board to build an isolation hospital, in agreement with the Greens. Raise Cottage opened as The Raise Hospital for Infectious Diseases the same year. In 1896 ten-year-old John Richard Bewley gives an account of his life in the 'Grasmere Fever Hospital' in *The West Cumberland Times*. Bewley describes the Hospital as 'a very exposed place and very far from everywhere.' He writes:

> We can see Grasmere valley and lake from our door. In summer we see many people passing on the coach road, some on foot, some in carriages, some on coaches, and some on bicycles. The hill leading from Grasmere is so steep that people have to walk up from the toll-bar, and they look very tired and hot and dusty and sometimes very cross when they get to the top.

On the death of Andrew Green in 1903, the land and the hospital erected on it were bequeathed to the Urban District Council. Andrew's will deferred delivery of this promise to his remaining brother James. However James died soon after Andrew. When the local board claimed sixty acres of ground it was James's widow Eliza who was left to clarify the intentions of the will. Arbitration settled the donation at a more reasonable three acres!

In 1947, the cottage was bought by the Achille Ratti Climbing Club. Established in 1942 by Bishop Thomas Bernard Pearson as an independent Catholic climbing club, Achille Ratti paid £799 for the building, but borrowed £1000 from the Lancaster Diocese to renovate it. Achille Ratti used the cottage as a climbing hut for the rest of the twentieth-century. A range of youth groups bedded down there as part of Achille Ratti's aim to foster a love of countryside.

In 2013, Achille Ratti sold the hut to free up capital to buy a property in the Wasdale valley. It has since been in private hands, but still runs as a hostel.

A distinctive 1950s AA phone box, a Grade II listed building in its own right, still stands in the layby adjacent to the property.

2. Toll Bar Cottage

Toll Bar Cottage lies at the North of what was Grasmere's toll road, half way up Dunmail Raise at Town Head. The toll road – or turnpike road – through the valley was built in 1775. *Black's Picturesque Guide to the Lake District* notes that the road rises gradually until it attains the height of 726 feet at the pass of Dunmail Raise.

The Ordnance Survey map of 1859 marks the location as Grasmere T.P. with a gate across the road and a building. This would have operated as such throughout the nineteenth century. The term turnpike refers to the military habit of blocking roadways with pikestaffs to control road traffic, with the pikestaff turning to permit passage.

The toll bar was the scene of paying taxes for travelling on the turnpike road. William Dickinson recalls the kind of mischief that some would attempt here in his 1875 book *Cumbriana*:

> Some years ago… at the turnpike gate between Grasmere and Dunmail Raise, the toll used to be taken by a good look-ing young matron to whom it was a pleasure pay the pence, were it only for the sake of her bright black eyes. One summer morning, a party of young men, on a walking ex-cursion to Keswick, were approaching this gate, when one of the company, who had some pretensions to the character of a wag, stept briskly out before the others to the open door of the toll-house, and called out "What have these fel-lows to pay?" The pretty toll taker hurried out and seeing nothing but a group of pedestrians, replied sharply "Nowte!" "Nowte," said the wit, staring up at the table of rates, "what, I see there's a charge for asses." "Yes," said she readily, "but there's nin for feuls, sooa thoo may gang on!"

From Eleanor Rawnsley's scrapbook, part of Phoebe Johnson's bequest to the Wordsworth Trust, we learn that the Grasmere Tolls from 1870-4 were kept by John Kirkby when the Toll was let to the highest bidder. The gate could be opened from one of the bedrooms.

	(1870)	(2019)
One pair of horses	1/-	£3.13
One horse vehicle with springs	6d	£1.57
Horse and Cart	4d	£1.04
The Mail Coach	free	
Other coaches per horse	6d	£1.57
Horse ridden	2d	52p
Return free if on the same day.		
A horse taken from the Wythburn smithy	free	

Mailcoach horses were kept at Town Head and were brought up the road by the lane, north of Broadrayne and changed there.

The building in 1965

3. Broadrayne

The name 'Broadrayne' traces back to the Old Norse words 'broad' (wide) and 'rein' (long strip). The farm sits above what would have been the flood plain of the valley and below the high fells behind the farm. Old maps and field walls indicate that the farm extended further to the north in a long strip. Whether people lived here or just used the land is hard to tell, but for the name to survive, something must have happened here for a very long time. The farm house stands on a large boulder base; there was probably an earlier building than the present house which dates to circa 1620 (it was a tradition to rebuild on the same site as the previous one). The stone walls around the farm and the shape of the fields also reflect a similar date. The farm deeds and a very early map indicate that these in-bye fields were enclosed before the 1720s.

The outlying barn to the north has always been known as the Bracken barn: the cut bracken was used for animal bedding and some of it was burnt to make potash, which was in turn made into soap to scour the grease from the wool before it was spun and sold. The building attached to the north of the farmhouse (now the Woolloft cottage), was the original cow byre with storage above for animal feed and the fleeces awaiting processing. The large Bank barn, recently converted and now known as 'The Yan', was built circa 1870-1880. This would have provided storage for hay, barley and oats on the top floor and a stable and shippon below for cows. The oats and barley were grown in the meadows further down the valley; no wheat could have been grown in the valley, as it is too wet. The Smithy is a detached one storey building that has now been converted to accommodation. It was at one time the blacksmith's workshop for the farm, from where it gets its name.

Broadrayne Farm has over the years bred some of the best sheep in the Lake District. The sheep you can often see round the farm are Lakeland Herdwicks. These sheep have been here for generations and are hefted to the farm. These are Broadrayne Sheep and are marked with the Broadrayne flock (Smit) mark. The photograph shows farm hands salving the sheep outside the building (now called The Byre) circa 1880. Salving involved waterproofing the sheep's fleece with a mixture of hot tar and rancid butter.

4. The Old Mill

The Old Mill, previously known as Mill Cottage, is a small stone-built cottage located a little outside the Village at the foot of Dunmail Raise. Constructed from a mixture of river and dressed stone, with a traditional slate roof, it looks towards Helm Crag, Silver How and Loughrigg over a patchwork of fields that were once used for growing corn. It is on the Coast to Coast Route leading up from the packhorse bridge at Lower Mill Bridge over Helvellyn to Patterdale. From Mill Lane you might think the building is a barn, as there are no windows in this elevation, However sharp eyes will spot evidence of an old loading bay now filled in, and an Ordnance Survey Bench Mark, both signs of its history.

The Mill Race, now moved from its original route, brings water from Tongue Ghyll, under the A591 and through a concrete rill. There are several other features in the property and the garden which reflect its history as a corn mill. A stone arch at lower ground level may have housed machinery, the remains of stone walls indicate possible storage sheds, and there is an infilled loading bay on the Mill Lane elevation. Inside there are old hooks in the ceiling of the living room. The walls are three feet thick and since the property stands at low level there is little noise from traffic.

A pencil drawing by Joseph Powell of Mill Cottage dated 1806 and entitled 'Near Grasmere' shows an overshot mill wheel where water was carried from the rill, through wooden troughs supported on trestles down to the waterwheel.

Joseph Powell, 'Near Grasmere' (1806)

Property deeds indicate that in 1915 Maria Walker of Lancrigg acquired Mill Cottage and the ruins of the Corn Mill. In 1919 Mill Cottage was bought by Eleanor Foster Rawnsley of Allan Bank. Subsequent owners were John Taylor of Helmside, then Kenneth Armstrong of Tongue Ghyll Cottage in 1925, Dorothy Armstrong in 1929, and in 1930 Frederick Henniker acquired it. In 1935 Sir Robert Benson Ewbank became the owner, letting it to Judith Marion Childe from Harrogate. Miss Childe purchased it in 1941, later leaving it to her niece Bridget Ann Johnson in her will. Bridget owned it until 1967 when it was sold for use as a holiday cottage to Mr. and Mrs. Douglas and Mr. and Mrs. Lyburn.

In 1970 it was sold again to Christopher and Nancy Cain who in 1987 sold it to their daughter and son in law, Judy and Peter Hitchcock.

The Old Mill has been in the family of the present owners for over fifty years. During that time a lady from Canada visited who left a note to say that her great grandparents had lived there in the 1880s with a family of eight children.

5. The Traveller's Rest

The Traveller's Rest is a sixteenth century coaching inn on the main road through Grasmere. It is a listed building with roughcast finish over stone rubble walls and a slate roof. Made up of two storeys in two blocks and stepped down the hillside, there are prominent sash windows and modern porches. The interior has visible oak beams and inglenooks.

The inn features in Canon Rawnsley's 1899 *Life and Nature at the English Lakes*:

> Here is the "Traveller's Rest," festooned by trails of the rich Tropeolum speciosum creeper. A pole-leaper is taking his traveller's rest, his great lance in hand; we shall see him on the field presently.

The current inn was built as an alehouse in the middle of the row of four terraced dwellings at the foot of Dunmail Raise. Whitwell, Mark & Co. Ltd of Kendal was the licensing brewery, which had been in business since 1757, and by the 1900s were a major employer in Highgate, Kendal (now the Brewery Arts Centre). As the adjacent cottages to The Traveller's became vacant each was bought by the

brewery to enlarge the business. The last tenant to leave the cottages was cartoonist Frank Hopkirk. Whitwell, Mark & Co. were bought out by Vaux brewery from Sunderland in 1946, followed by Jennings.

To comply with licensing regulations, and in order to have a spirit licence the car park to the north had to be created, thus losing the greater part of the garden.

In the mid twentieth-century, Claude Harrison painted a new sign for the Traveller's Rest, shown here. Harrison had studios in Grasmere and Ambleside at various times, and also painted the sign for The Swan hotel (a version of which still adorns the hotel at the end of Swan Lane today).

It is at present in private hands.

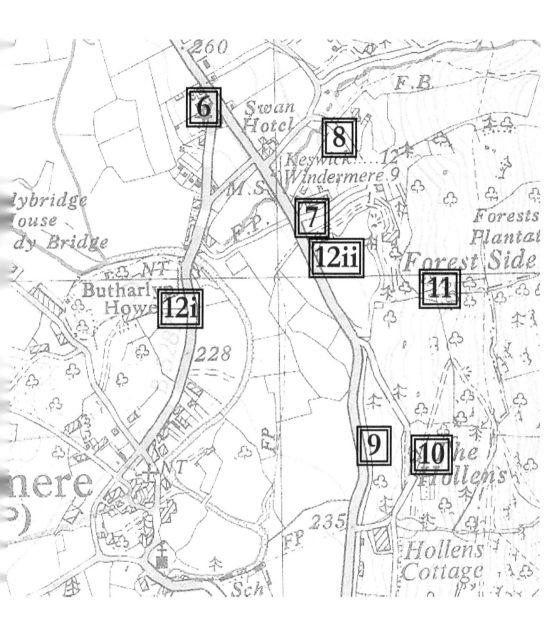

6.	Great Cross Cottages	10.	The Hollens
7.	Our Lady of the Wayside	11.	Forest Side
8.	Michael's Croft	12.i	Broadgate Orchard
9.	Grove Cottage	12.ii	Greenhead Fold

6. Great Cross Cottages

Sir Frederick William Chance (1852-1932) lived in Carlisle where he ran a manufacturing firm, but he had a second home at Lancrigg in Grasmere. He was a Liberal MP and sat in the House of Commons from 1905-1910. He was Mayor of Carlisle in 1904 and the High Sherriff of Cumberland in 1915.

Sir Frederick and his wife Mary Seaton Chance lost two sons in the First World War. As a memorial to their tragic loss the houses at Great Cross Trust were built.

When the cottages were built and let Sir Frederick Chance gave the rent from the cottages to Grasmere Village School to provide two scholarships to Kelsick Grammar School. We know that Marjorie Dodgson (nee Hodgson) – born in 1914 and an interesting village character, whose son later became one of the Great Cross trustees – was one of the village children fortunate enough to receive a scholarship from this endowment.

The houses were built in an area of the village on land that had previously been stables belonging to Bruce Rigg. According to a register of the fields of Grasmere the field was called Great Cross, hence the name given to estate. It is thought that the first two houses to be built were the ones that front onto the road that is now the A591: these cottages have a memorial plaque visible. Next to be built were four directly behind the front ones and finally the two that face towards Loughrigg, making eight in total.

In 1982 Miss Mary Chance, the granddaughter of Sir Frederick Chance, gifted the properties to the Grasmere Village Society because she wanted to ensure that the properties were kept for the use of local people. The ownership of the cottages had been passed down through the family with Miss Chance holding the deeds since 1975. Miss Chance, a resident of Carlisle, felt that with no close relatives living in Cumbria, there would be no one to oversee the care of the properties after her death. Traditionally the properties were for the use of old servants and local people such as the district nurse. Miss Chance felt that by gifting the properties to the Village Society this tradition would be able to be maintained.

The Grasmere Village Society had more than 300 members at the time of the bequest and the secretary, Mrs. Elizabeth Braithwaite, explained that the properties would be managed by six trustees appointed by the Village Society with a contract being signed to ensure that they cannot be bought or let as holiday cottages.

The first Declaration of Trust was drawn up on 20th July 1982.

On 17th May 2003 a new Trust was drawn up intended to replace the 1982 Declaration of Trust. In this declaration it is clear that the Great Cross Trust is registered as a Charity with the Charities Commission.

In 2016 three more cottages were built on the land at Great Cross, named The Chance Cottages in acknowledgement of Sir Frederick Chance's benevolence. The building project was funded from the Trust's own accumulated resources plus a loan from the Grasmere Rothay Trust, a grant from the South Lakeland District Council's second home fund and finally by a mortgage with the Trust's bankers. No other monies were contributed from local sources. It is interesting to note from the records, that 'because being a Social Landlord and not a Housing Association the Trust did not qualify for Housing Corporation finance'.

When writing about the building of these houses Mrs. Elizabeth Braithwaite MBE wrote in 2008:

> There are five Trustees governing this Housing Trust who all take their responsibilities extremely seriously. It needs foresight, courage and any amount of perseverance to bring projects like this to completion.

Two of the cottages in 1965

7. Our Lady of the Wayside

Our Lady of the Wayside R.C. Church, 'Madonna Della Strada,' was the first Catholic Church to be built in Grasmere since the Reformation. The foundation stone was laid in July 1964 by Right Reverend Bernard Foley, Bishop of Lancaster.

Dean Reverend George Atkinson had said weekly Mass at Dale Lodge Hotel Since his arrival in the village in the late 1930s, but increasing numbers of tourists prompted the decision to erect a permanent church. Mrs. Alice 'Granny' Baillie of Ben Place Hotel donated the land, and parishioners raised £10,000 of the £23,000 required for the build. A memorial book near the altar lists the names of all those who contributed. Architect Wilfrid C. Mangan of Preston designed the simple cruciform church which seats 120, and it was built by T. Armstrong & Sons of Cockermouth.

The altar was consecrated by Right Reverend T.B. Pearson, Bishop of Sinda on 12th August, 1965. Relics of Saints Christiani and Laurentia were sealed in the altar stone which is made of local green slate, as are the Stations of the Cross. Above the altar an unusual painted canopy depicts the Trinity breaking through the stars. On Sunday 15th August 1965 (the feast of the Assumption of Our Lady) Bishop Foley officiated at the solemn blessing and opening ceremony which was attended by clergymen representing local Anglican and Methodist churches as well as hundreds of worshippers, many of whom listened to the service broadcast on loudspeakers outside the church. In his sermon, Monsignor Smith of Carlisle recalled the Christian practice of erecting wayside shrines on dangerous mountain passes. He celebrated this new wayside shrine for travellers to stop, rest and be thankful at the foot of Dunmail Raise.

With few resident parishioners, the church was built mainly for the benefit of visitors, on whose generosity it depended. Renowned composer and conductor John Rutter of Cambridge wrote in the Visitors' Book on 1st June 2001 'Lovely church – should have a better organ'. His recommendation was realised in 2008 when Grasmere's Methodist church closed, and its superior organ was donated to Our Lady's.

Six more semi-retired senior priests followed Reverend Atkinson: Reverends Corbishley, Roney, Kershaw, Harrison, Buxton and finally Duane, officiating between them at a total of 52 baptisms, 23 funerals and 186 weddings. In its picture perfect setting, it is no surprise that the church was a popular choice for weddings, which brought in substantial and much-needed income for the parish.

In 2008, facing dwindling mass attendance and a shortage of priests, the Diocese of Lancaster published its 'Fit for Mission' document, reviewing parish activity and outlining draft proposals for the future of its parishes. Our Lady's merged with Mater Amabilis in Ambleside, and only a handful of resident parishioners, all retirees, regularly attended Mass at Our Lady's. Visitors in holiday season swelled the numbers attending Sunday Mass to between 50 and 100. When Reverend Fr. David Duane, already aged over 80, retired on 25th August 2013, the church was closed to the public. It remains furnished and available for private worship to clergy and religious occupying the adjacent Wayside Bungalow, and there is still hope that it will reopen for public celebration of Mass in the future.

8. Michael's Croft

On the fell side between Forest Side to the south and Broadrayne to the north, split by Greenhead Gill, are a number of place name references to 'Michael'. These include Michael's Nook, Michael's Fold and Michael's Croft.

It is very probable that these were named after the shepherd hero in Wordsworth's famous pastoral poem 'Michael'. It is also possible that Wordsworth himself named his shepherd Michael after the immediate area then known as Michael-place (as recorded in the Grasmere Parish Register of 1688). The vicinity was possibly named after Michael Knott, owner of Broadrayne at that time. Wordsworth walked this fell side extensively.

Michael's Croft began life as a modest bungalow on an extensive field plot below Michael's Fold, built in the 1960s. This field plot had extensive panoramic views from Butter Crag to Loughrigg and across to Silver How, Easedale and Helm Crag. Part of this large field plot was subsequently split into a further two neighbouring plots in the 1980s, again with pleasant bungalow constructions added.

Michael's Croft had some relatively minor modifications and enhancements, changing ownership a couple of times. Then controversy hit. In late 2009, plans were submitted to the National Park for the complete demolition of the existing property, to be replaced by arguably one of the most radical new buildings in the parish.

Designed by leading local architect Ben Cunliffe, the proposed building was to feature not a traditional green slate roof, but two angular steel roofs, split by a sloping glazed central atrium. The ground floor to the rear was to be glazed floor-to-ceiling, with two cantilevered balconies extending out over the glazing. As an interpretation of contemporary Lakeland, the house would be partially clad in slate and hardwood, and finished in a self-cleaning modern white render. It would also be technologically advanced and energy efficient with a geo-thermal heat pump sourcing energy from three bore holes each drilled to 300 feet below ground.

The key question was whether such a radical and controversial design – not just for Grasmere but for the wider National Park – would get planning permission? The plans were certainly in line with the emerging policy to support new and exciting architecture within the National Park. The answer was yes, even avoiding the need for appeals and resubmissions. It seems the planners were indeed receptive to sympathetic cutting edge design and architecture, even in this most revered of villages.

The new Michael's Croft was built and finalised in 2012 and was subsequently shortlisted for architectural awards. It is a building that still generates much debate and discussion. It is certainly a unique landmark building, clearly visible from the summits of Loughrigg and Silver How.

9. Grove Cottage

Grove Cottage, sometimes referred to as The Grove, was built c.1690 according to the church records, probably as a farm building on the Hollens Estate. It is rubble built into a hill using any stones found lying about. The walls are one metre wide at the base tapering to 70 cm at the roof. The lintel over the cellar door demonstrates local architecture of the time. The cellar would have been an animal shelter or farm storage. The oak lintel above the blocked in window on the front of the cottage, now covered by roses and honeysuckle, is about 500 years old and would have been used in some other building originally. Likewise, the main oak beams within the cottage could have been salvaged from ships or an old barn as they have many notches cut in them. Nothing went to waste in those days.

It is first identifiable in Dorothy Wordsworth's journal when she refers to walking 'up past Lewthwaites'. The Lewthwaite family consisted of George, a waller, his wife Ann, and daughters Barbara (b. 1791) and Hannah (b. 1794). Hannah was given work as helper to the Wordsworths with their babies John and Dora. When writing his poem 'The Pet Lamb', Wordsworth used the image he had of Barbara at play as inspiration, but Barbara's vanity about this was something he regretted.

The Garnetts and Valentines, both wallers/stonemasons, occupied the cottage for the rest of the nineteenth century and their descendants are still living in Grasmere today.

As part of The Hollens Estate it was purchased in 1881 by the Manchester Corporation, as precursor to the Thirlmere Reservoir Project and an Indenture was signed between the Corporation and the Harwards.

In her 1911 book *The Church of Grasmere* Mary Armitt mentions that along the presumed line of the Roman road at high level between White Moss and the Dunmail Raise 'it is interesting to find there exists a line of scattered homesteads; while the modern road below was, until the recent spurt in building, vacant but for a cottage and the Swan Inn.' The cottage could only be Grove Cottage.

In 1954 Grove Cottage was offered freehold to the sitting tenants Edward James Wilson, painter and decorator, and his wife Emily Sophia Wilson for £1850. Grove Cottage was then called The Grove. Edward James Wilson had a mortgage of £1400 from Keswick Building Society.

10. The Hollens

Hollens is taken from the Old English word 'holegn' meaning holly.

In the late eighteenth century Mr. and Mrs. John Olive lived at the house, known then as 'The Hollins'. After their departure for Usk in 1802, Thomas King Esquire, a rich farmer from Cossington, Leicestershire, moved to the Hollins. A watercolour painting by William Green in 1813 shows a very fine house. Thomas King felled the lovely birch trees featured in the painting and replaced them with young larches in straight lines, upsetting William Wordsworth. In 1823, King rented out what was by then called Hollins Grove.

In 1841 Ralph Henry Alcock bought the Hollins estate. Alcock gave his name to Alcock Tarn, 1000 feet above Grasmere village on the western flanks of Heron Pike. Alcock enlarged the existing natural tarn, known as Butter Crags, by means of a small stone and earth dam to create a trout lake. In 1848, Alcock let the Hollins as a family hotel, called The Hollins Inn and Lowther Hotel. John Mawson was the first to run the building as a hotel.

In the 1851 census it was called 'Hollins and Lowther Hotel', owned by Edward Brown, Innkeeper and Auctioneer. Living with him were his wife Jane, children Mary, Edward and Sarah Jane plus four servants and a post boy. Edward Brown went on to employ Levi Hodgson to build Brown's Hotel (see **Daffodil Hotel** entry) on the shore of the lake.

Somewhere within the extensive grounds there is a well of good repute. It had been examined by an expert in 1843 when an effort was made to establish a hydropathic cure in Grasmere. The water was pronounced finer than the better-known St. Oswald's well, but the owner of the land at the time would not sell.

In 1869 'The Hollens' was put up for sale. It was divided up into seventeen Lots, the mansion house being Lot 1. By 1870 John Harward, a solicitor, owned the Hollens. This was the time when the Thirlmere reservoir was being suggested as a means of getting water to Manchester as the city had outgrown its own reservoirs of drinking water. As the aquaduct tunnel would be passing through the local countryside the landowners set up the Thirlmere Defence Association to oppose it. The Association was led by John Harward who it was said 'was more concerned about the disturbance he would suffer while the aqueduct was being constructed'. The aquaduct tunnel would pass through 570 yards of his 172 acre estate and would only be 160 yards from the house. He refused to sell the land. Eventually he changed his mind and decided he would be able to sell the estate for £26,000 and £2000 for expenses incurred by the Thirlmere Defence Association. There was one condition he had to fulfil. He must sever all connections with the Association. Thus the land passed to the Manchester Corporation.

Miss E.A. Harward, 'The Hollins' (1850s)

John Harward died on June 23rd 1879 at the Hollens. The Estate was not sold back into the public domain until 1924 when Edward Lawrence of Wigan bought it for £6850.

In 1946 Ken Sykes bought the Hollens and turned it back into a successful hotel. Today the National Trust uses the building as its North West Headquarters, under the name Lake District Consultancy Hub. It has had quite a few alterations since 1813.

THE HOLLENS HOTEL

Grasmere Publicity Association Advert, 1964

11. Forest Side

Until 1852 the area known as Forest Side was farmland, housing a cluster of buildings, including a smithy, barns, pig pens and ostler's accommodation. 'Fforrest syd' cottage is mentioned in the earliest Grasmere church register in 1611. This housed the ostler who worked for the Swan Hotel on the north-south carriage route. Forest Side Cottage (now Fir Tree Cottage) and adjacent barn building still exist today.

In 1853 the Forest Side house was built, more or less as we see it today, by Stephen Heelis, a solicitor from the north of England. He was responsible for building the walled garden. Until recently there was evidence of a coal shute leading from the path on the fell side above Forest Side down the steep slope to the outhouses at the back of the main building.

Heelis's wife died in 1858 and the property was then sold to a James Harrison, purchase price £7000. The Heelis family are buried in Grasmere Churchyard. Stephen Heelis died in 1871.

By 1863, Charles Younge, a silversmith from Sheffield, owned Forest Side. Younge was married in April of that year, aged 70, to Emily Barker, aged 20, from Huddersfield. Emily and Charles had

Sanderson and Dixon Postcard, 1960s

one daughter, Edith, born in 1864. Charles died aged 74 and there is a memorial in the church to him. Emily continued at Forest Side until 1888 when it was put up for auction. The auction gives a sense of the house and its ground at that time, incorporating a coach house, stables, two cottages, walled kitchen garden, conservatory and vinery, grounds of fifty acres with a noble stand of trees and shrubs leading to the carriage entrance. The house did not sell and was again auctioned in 1897, and sold to Edmond Brownhill, Justice of the Peace. He died in 1914, after seventeen years' ownership.

Forest Side was then owned by William Duncan until 1925 when ownership was registered to Thomas Dixon. In 1929, the new owner was the Co-operative Holidays Association (later the Countrywide Holidays Association) whose aim was to provide rural holidays for working-class people. Forest Side later became an hotel. After a refurbishment in 2014, the beautiful grounds and buildings are once again a place of splendour. In 2016, the Forest Side was awarded a Michelin star.

12. Broadgate Orchard and Greenhead Fold

Broadgate Orchard (2013) and Greenhead Fold (2018) are two recently built affordable housing schemes in Grasmere.

Although affordable housing is a national issue, it has been recognised for many years now that the issue is of particular concern in the Lake District National Park. The founding of the Lakeland Housing Trust (formerly known as the Lake Country Cottage Society) in 1937 illustrates that provision of homes for local people was an issue before the Second World War. Responding to a shortage of houses for workers and their families the trust still owns properties in Grasmere today, providing rented accommodation at a low cost.

From the mid-1960s onwards, the proportion of second home and holiday home ownership within the National Park has increased dramatically, with high demand leading to higher prices. In addition, local wages within the rural and tourism sectors are low, leading to a wide gap between local incomes and house prices. House price to income ratios are irreconcilable.

In Grasmere the issue is particularly acute, with estimations that over 50% of the existing housing stock is either used as second homes and/or as holiday lets. Although Grasmere has a thriving local community, this high ratio can have significant implications on the village.

Affordable housing attempts to meet the needs of local eligible households, including the availability of housing at a cost low enough for them to afford. Simply put, it enables locals who want to stay local, to stay local.

Despite being a relatively small community, and after significant consultation, Grasmere has had two sites recently developed for affordable housing. In 2013, the Broadgate Orchard scheme of fifteen dwellings was completed on the site of the former kitchen garden of the Youth Hostel in the centre of Grasmere village, within the Conservation Area. Although traditional in form, the buildings have a modern design. The dwellings have some traditional design elements, such as local slated pitched roof and overhanging eaves, and also exhibit modern detailing including zinc flat roof dormers, timber panelled window surrounds, and larger amounts of glazing.

In 2018, the Greenhead Fold scheme of eleven dwellings was completed on a small field of scrub land adjacent to the Swan Hotel (and formerly owned by the Hotel). This was a particularly challenging site running along side Greenhead Gill which had been subject to landslide damage at various locations from Storm Desmond. Again, these dwellings were designed to sympathetically fit the locality.

Greenhead Fold in 2019

Building affordable housing within the National Park is undoubtedly challenging and not without controversy. Identifying and purchasing land, meeting planning constraints and complexities, holding extensive local consultations, covering additional construction costs (such as slate roofs and render restrictions) all make it difficult for schemes to be viable and genuinely affordable for local people. However it is remarkable that Grasmere has recently managed to develop two distinct sites and build twenty-six new dwellings for affordable housing.

Broadgate Orchard in 2019

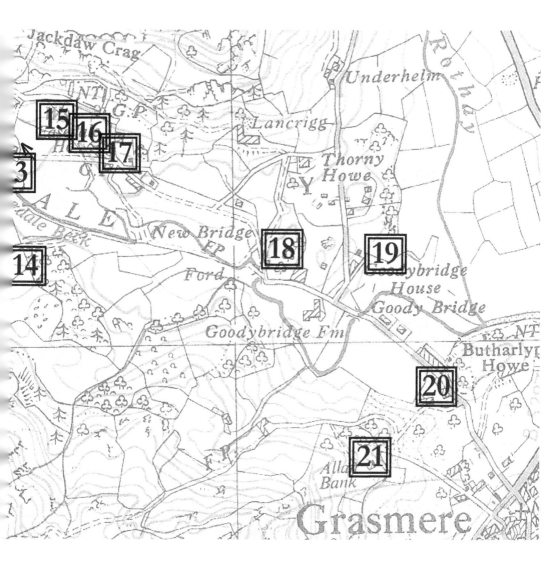

13. Easedale
    Refreshment Hut
14. Blindtarn
15. Easedale House
16. Jackdaw Cottage
17. Kitty Crag

18. Stubdale Cottage
19. Goody Bridge House
20. Glenthorne, Bankside
    and Fieldside Cottages
21. Allan Bank

13. Easedale Refreshment Hut

The stone building that became the Easedale Refreshment Hut was built by Robert Hodgson in 1858, possibly replacing an earlier turf-built shepherd's hut. A huge boulder was incorporated and formed one wall. Building on common land, Hodgson paid five shillings yearly rent.

Robert Hayton took the building on in 1866. Hayton's daughter, Ann, married William Wilson in the same year. William Wilson was the grandson of the Wilsons who ran the Swan Hotel in the early nineteenth century, and was known to many as Swanny Wilson. His occupation is usually given as contractor and mountain guide.

Together the family started a refreshment business in the hut. Garnett's *Guide to the English Lake District* (1870) reports 'there is a boat for hire on the tarn and near it a hut where a humble refreshment may be had.'

On Hayton's death in 1888, the hut was let to his daughter, Ann Wilson, still at 5/- a year, payable to the Grasmere Commoners. The business, advertised as Tourists' Rest, flourished under Ann and her husband William, becoming famous for its bacon and eggs. Plain Tea was then 1s 0d., whereas Ham and Eggs would set you back 1s 6d. In today's money that would mean £4.10 for Plain Tea and £6.15 for Ham and Eggs. Very reasonable considering that supplies were all carried up by the Wilsons or their pony ('cuddy').

Canon Rawnsley wrote of Robert Hayton:

> 'Age fell upon him. He could no longer take the upward climb, but still he would be seen on the back of his noble 'cuddy', and here he would spend not only long days but long nights, till the cuddy returned to take him to his weekend home.'

Photographs taken after the turn of the century show the hut was well appointed. The outbreak of the First World War in 1914 and William's death in 1918 heralded inevitable change, but the business continued through the inter-war years with various owners. One, Michael O'Brien, entertained visitors by bending six-inch nails with his hands into fantastic shapes. In the 1930s a couple from Rydal ran the hut, bringing their supplies on the bus to Grasmere, and carried them up to the tarn.

After the Second World War the hut fell into disrepair and was finally dismantled by the National Park Voluntary Wardens. The site, and the large boulder which was part of the building, can still be seen. The path up is not a 'gentle stroll,' but a genuine fell walk up to 915ft.

Swanny Wilson inside the Tourists' Rest with Visitors Book

Charlotte M. Fletcher, 'Hut on Common Land' (1890)

14. Blindtarn

Blindtarn is an isolated Grade II listed cottage and two barns situated at the upper end of Low Easedale. It is first recorded as Blintarne Gyll in St. Oswalds church register in 1572. There are also records of a John Benson of Blintarn Gill having children baptised in 1574 and 1577.

Circumstantial evidence suggests that it is highly likely that the cottage was built to support the processing of woollen cloth at the sparsely documented fulling mill in Blindtarn Gill or possibly the well known one at Sourmilk Gill which is 600m away. The Bensons were a very successful and extended family of fullers first recorded in Grasmere in 1486.

The cottage is the only building situated on the south side of Easedale and is hence much less favoured by the sun, particularly in winter, so its siting was determined by other priorities. The building is of a rubble construction using predominantly field stones. It was originally a single or two room dwelling with storage in the roof space accessed by external stone steps to the rear, the remains of which were still visible until recently. The adjoining stable was probably added later. There is a spice cupboard, fire beam and fire window indicating the previous use of an open hearth fire. Two unusual features are several stone shelves built into the walls and a stone pillar supporting one end of the fire beam. At some point, presumably in the nineteenth century, fireplaces were installed in the main room and two upstairs rooms to enable the burning of coal rather than peat. Two small dormer windows were also added.

Blindtarn is best known locally for its association with the Wordsworth family. It was the home of George and Sarah Green who died returning from the Langdales on a wintery night in January 1807, leaving behind eight children. One daughter was in service with the Wordsworth family at Allan Bank and Dorothy Wordsworth became involved in starting and administering a fund for the education and placement of the children. Dorothy wrote an account of the tragedy and subsequent events called 'A Narrative concerning George and Sarah Green of the Parish of Grasmere'. It was also the subject of Wordsworth's 'Elegiac Stanzas Composed in the Churchyard of Grasmere'.

In 1959 Blindtarn was purchased by Philip and Anthea Craggs for £2250, from James Elleray, the farmer at nearby Brimmer Head. The building was in a very dilapidated condition requiring a complete renovation, including fitting a staircase and converting the stable into a kitchen and bathroom. Unfortunately the, presumably original, slate floor and floorboards were replaced. They subsequently converted one of the barns into a two bedroom cottage. After they moved to Kendal in 1970 Blindtarn became a holiday home for the family, friends and paying guests. In 2016 their daughter, her husband and children moved in to make it a family home once again. Another refurbishment was completed in 2019 adding a large living room and new bathroom. Fragments of a newspaper and poster were found in the upper walls dating from the late nineteenth century suggesting a possible date for the conversion of the upper floor to bedrooms. Additional stone shelving and several blocked up windows and doors were also revealed.

Another recent discovery was of two high quality glass negatives of the house dated 1902 and 1905. Deborah Walsh of the Armitt Museum has said the handwriting on one of the sleeves indicates it was taken by Herbert Bell, the well known Ambleside photographer.

15. Easedale House

The story of Easedale House begins around 450 million years ago, when an arc of four volcanic islands form off the coast of the continent of Avalonia. Grasmere's position is on the edge of one of the islands, the 'Scafell caldera', but after a short series of eruptions the crater collapses and fills with water. Into the lake washes volcanic ash and debris that becomes compressed into sharp beds of 'volcanistic sandstone'. It is this distinctive red rock (what the British Geological Survey terms the Pavey Ark Member) that forms most of Easedale House and many other 'red' buildings in the village, probably mined from Jackdaw Crag quarries just 150 yards behind the house. Higher up are grey-green volcanic tuffs interbedded with andesite sills that provide the lintels and quoins.

At the conclusion of the Ordovician, approximately 400 million years ago, Laurentia, carrying Scotland, crumpled our 'Cumbrian' islands and a by-product of all the heat and pressure was metamorphic rock such as the slate on Easedale's roof, probably mined from the caves near Rydal. A Silurian sea surrounded the new mountains and sediments – the Windermere Supergroup – were laid down unconformably, including Brathay Blue mudstones that became the large smooth slates found in the kitchen floor and worktops of Easedale House.

There are suggestions of a property on this site in 1331 and 1654, and maps from 1770 and 1828 indicate a house. It is unclear which of these relate to Easedale House or the cottage on the same site, now

known as Jackdaw Cottage. Various spellings of Easedale are present in the record, e.g. Asedale; Esdall; Aysedale and Aisdale. National Trust archives suggest that the stables were once part of Jackdaw Cottage but there seems to be a house, probably the 'farmhouse-style' east wing, by the first half of the nineteenth century. There are records of a Reverend Edward Rowlandson owning land in Easdale.

In 1811 the house was bought by George Dixon of 'Aysdale'. When George Dixon died in 1846 the freehold was left to his daughter, Diana Fleming, who sold it on to John Tyson (a taxman from Aberystwyth). It was John who probably extended the house considerably, adding the more stately south-facing wing. By 1870 local William Wilkinson was able to describe how 'the old Dwellinghouse has been converted into ... the present Mansion House called Easdale House'.

In 1870 John Tyson died and the house appears to be sold to Jane Fleming and then to Reverend H.M. Fletcher, Rector of Grasmere 1878-93. His daughter, Charlotte, wrote the first Grasmere dialect plays and her artwork features throughout this book.

Easedale House was sold in 1891 to W. H. Hills. In this period there are mentions of Easedale House in George Fothergill's diary (see **Allan Bank** entry), detailing how in 1884 Easedale House was used as an isolation ward for children with scarlet fever. On another occasion, a party was dispatched to help to clear the drains – nothing changes!

His daughter, Christine. D. Hills, owned Easedale House from 1909 until her death in 1952. She bequeathed both the house and the cottage to the National Trust, who rent it out. The accomplished painter Claude Harrison (1922-2009, see **The Traveller's Rest** entry) was a long-term tenant of Easedale House and some of his 'etchings' are still visible on the attic ceilings. Laurence Harwood OBE, as regional director of the National Trust, lived at Easedale for 25 years and did much to improve the gardens. The Jackman family moved in in 2004. The UK national standards for Sustainable Development and Sustainable Communities were both drafted in the house. The international (ISO 37101/104) standards for communities that followed were completed at a conference in Grasmere in 2015, part hosted by The Wordsworth Trust. National frameworks for successful rural communities are now underway, based on Grasmere.

16. Jackdaw Cottage

Jackdaw Cottage, originally called Easedale Cottage, resides in the grounds of Easedale House. On the lower floor, the kitchen and sitting room are fitted with slate floors. The sitting room is overlooked by a beamed ceiling. At one end of the cottage is an old stable with cobbled floors and an original nail-studded door. A trap door in the ceiling connects the stable to the hayloft, once used for dropping down hay when needed. The upper floor has two bedrooms with windows overlooking the valley. A heather drying platform is also found on the upper floor.

The cottage was built around 1700 and little is known about the early owners. A spice cupboard originally in the cottage bears the inscription 'I G 1708'. A built-in press cupboard in the sitting room also holds the inscription of 'I G E 1735', which suggest either the

George Sheridan Knowles, 'Easedale Cottage' (1882)

Green or Grigg families, both of whom were known in Easedale at the time.

In 1829 the cottage was owned by Agnes Walker. Her father owned it before her and ran it as an inn for pack-horse drivers travelling to and from Borrowdale.

Whilst they lived in Easedale House, the Hills family rented Easedale Cottage out. At the turn of the century Mrs Grisedale was their tenant, occupying Easedale Cottage and notably entering her hounds 'Crazy Jane' and 'Backbarrow War Lad' in the Grasmere Sports Hound Trail in 1898 and 1901 respectively. When Christine Hills died, she left both the house and cottage to the National Trust.

Caroline Morland, 'Cottage in Easedale, Aggy Walker's 1824-1836'

17. Kitty Crag

The present house was constructed in the 1850s. However, there had been a cottage on the site since the early nineteenth century, owned by Edward Dixon. When he died in 1830 it was sold to William Wilson, who bequeathed it to his son John Wilson of Staveley in 1849. He rented the property to the Harrison family. The cottage, garden, barn (Bouthwaite Barn) and orchard were advertised for sale in 1850 as eligible for the erection of villa residences. Development of the site must have commenced soon after the sale.

By the 1860s it was the property of John Davy, the husband of Margaret Fletcher whose mother Elizabeth Fletcher had lived at Lancrigg until her death in 1858. John Davy qualified as a doctor, joined the Army Medical Department and eventually rose to become the Inspector General of Army Hospitals. There is no evidence that John and Margaret lived at Kitty Crag: they had built a house, Lesketh How, between Ambleside and Rydal and moved there in 1845.

Kitty Crag remained in the ownership of descendants of John and Margaret until 1922 when Sir Humphry Davy Rolleston, John and Margaret's grandson, sold the house. Sir Humphry was a prominent physician and for nine years was Physician in Ordinary to King George V.

During the Davy/Rolleston ownership the house was rented out, and it saw a succession of tenants, some of whom were only seasonal visitors. These seasonal visitors travelled from highly populated urban areas such as Preston, Liverpool and London to enjoy the idyllic surroundings of Kitty Crag.

With the change of ownership in 1922 Kitty Crag became owner-occupied. The new owner, Mary Elizabeth Paley, was the daughter of E. G. Paley of Paley and Austin, the renowned architectural practice based in Lancaster. She lived in the house for a number of years before moving to Cartmel. In 1939 the house was sold to Margaret Price-Heywood and although she died in 1947 her husband remained in the property until he sold in 1964 to Isabel and Stanley James. However, Basil Price-Heywood did not remove far: he converted the barn in the grounds to a residence, now known as Bouthwaite Barn, as accommodation for himself.

The new owner, Isabel James, was an innovative businesswoman: by the late 1940s she ran two successful vegetarian guest houses in the village, Beck Allans and Rothay Bank. She became the national secretary of the Vegetarian Catering Association and published a number of leaflets publicising the vegetarian and vegan cause. In 1976 she gifted some of the woodland behind the house to the National Trust. In 1981 the house was sold to Robert and Elaine Harvey. Kitty Crag's involvement with the vegetarian cause re-emerged in the 1990s when then owners, Robert and Janet Whittington used the house as an annex to their vegetarian hotel at Lancrigg, in the house originally inhabited by Mrs. Fletcher.

18. Stubdale Cottage

In 1851 Edward Wilson, joiner and builder in Grasmere, bought a piece of land at Stubdale in the Easedale Valley on which he subsequently built the present Easedale Lodge. He apparently already owned, and probably lived in, the older southern part of Stubdale Cottage and his joiner's shop was attached to it. Edward's wife Hannah died in 1855.

Stubdale Cottage was subsequently owned by Mrs. Dalston and then Mr. and Mrs. Hayton, who both let rooms to tourists. Richard Hayton was a postman for the village, and had a hand in two buildings (see **Easedale Refreshment Hut** and **Harley's** entries). In 1920 the property was bought by Albert Heyworth of Alderley Edge, Cheshire who converted the joiner's shop into a northward extension of the original Stubdale Cottage as a house for himself in about 1921.

In the late 1930s, the Mack family lived here. Charles Mack was a mechanical engineer. In 1955, Harold Birch lived at Stubdale Cottage, and was left a small sum of money on the death of his friend and near neighbour, the novelist Miss Edith Marjorie Ward (of Crag Foot).

In 1963 the property and adjacent cottage were bequeathed to the National Trust by Mr. and Mrs. Henry Walter Moberley. Mrs. Moberley continued to live there after her husband's demise until her own death in the 1970s. The Moberleys used the property as a guest house for many of their friends over the years including such eminent visitors as Lord Justice Denning and Lord Hunt, famous as the leader of the 1953 British Everest expedition.

Stubdale Cottage is chiefly regarded as architecturally important for the 1920s alterations, forming an extremely good example of an interior of that date. The most important features are: circular chimney stacks, slate porches, slate sconces in the pantry and slate floors; staircases, inglenook fireplace in living room and interior woodwork. The walls are of surface gathered and quarried slate with rough upright quoins and slate sills and lintels to openings, windows having arched voussoirs. The roof is of local slates laid in diminishing courses with sandstone ridge tiles supported by a structure of one king post truss of sawn softwood. Two rolled steel trusses of Lanarkshire Steel support the northern section of the roof. A late nineteenth century garage stands just to the north west of Stubdale Cottage and attached to its northern side is an early lean-to former earth closet.

STUBDALE COTTAGE. GRASMERE.

Phoebe May-Johnson, from 'Snap Shots' photographic album

19. Goody Bridge House

Old documents refer to 'Goody Bridge' as a district including Goody Bridge House, High Goody Bridge (aka Goody Bridge Farm), Goody Bridge Cottage (now Low Fold) and Stubdale.

Goody Bridge House is a Grade II* listed building, being a typical seventeenth century Lake District farmhouse. The exact date of building is unknown as the old deeds have been lost. There was once a date stone for 1699. This probably refers to the front of the house, which appears to have been built at right angles onto an older building (now the kitchen). The back of the house has older large, thick irregular roof slates, smaller windows (one with tiny irregular panes set in lead) and a cylindrical chimney stack. The later chimney stacks are rectangular with paired sloping slates protecting the chimney pots. There are lines of drip-stones over the windows (including one over a presumed blocked-up fire window) and iron gutter supports (redundant at the front as the roof here has been raised at some stage). An attached single story out-building was once a cattle byre-cum-dairy and has alcoves for bee-hives built into the front wall.

In 1744 an Edwin Green (1664-1747) wrote a will which mentions his residence at 'Guddy Bridge, Grasmere'. Edwin has many connections to branches of the Green family of Grasmere. The annotated field maps of 1847 show that Goody Bridge House was owned by John Wilson (b. 1776) who is recorded in the censuses of 1851 and 1861

as living there with his daughters Ann Wilson (b. 1806) and Jane Wilson (b. 1811) and Ann's daughter, Mary Green Wilson (b. 1840). Ann died in 1880 and Jane died in 1882, leaving Goody Bridge House to her nephew Joseph Youdell (the son of John Wilson's daughter Sarah) for his lifetime and thereafter to his son, John Wilson Youdell (b. 1874).

Joseph was a Langdale farmer and one time proprietor of both Dungeon Ghyll hotels. He never lived at Goody Bridge, but rented it out.

One known tenant was Walter Baldry, son of well-known Grasmere residents William and Louise Baldry. Other tenants were the  Borwicks and Moffats. After Joseph Youdell's death John Wilson Youdell took possession of Goody Bridge House in 1925 and lived and farmed there with his wife, Mary (née Thompson) and family until his death in 1958. The family of the current owner bought the house from Wilson Youdell's executors in 1962.

Typical seventeenth century features in the house include: staircase with turned balusters and panelled newel posts, spice cupboards, an oak-panelled partition and some original doors and windows.

The adjacent barn is older than the house and is also Grade II* listed. It is of cruck-beam construction in a mediaeval style as is seen in other old barns in the district. It has two original pairs of crucks, the third pair and half the roof having been destroyed in a fire (probably the fire reported in the *Westmorland Gazette* in 1868) and repaired with Victorian materials. The old part of the roof which was in a poor state was re-roofed in 1997 using the original large, thick, graduated slates. Tie beams which had been sawn off at some time were also replaced. The central part of the floor is a threshing floor covered with smooth, flat slate slabs. A small winnowing door is placed opposite the main door.

High Goody Bridge (aka Goody Bridge Farm) is also of seventeenth century origin and shows typical features at the back, though the front has more recent modifications so it is not listed. It has a large attached barn and a smaller, probably older barn or byre at the rear. The latter has now been converted into a cottage.

The house now known as Low Fold is situated behind Goody Bridge Farm. It is of similar date and also has a large barn.

20. Glenthorne, Bankside and Fieldside Cottages

Glenthorne was built in 1834 by the owner of Allan Bank at the time, Mr. Dawson, and started life as a 'two up, two down' cottage serving as the lodge to Allan Bank. It was occupied by Mr. Dawson's coachman. There was a toll bar outside the cottage on Easedale Road which at that time was a cart track leading up to Easedale village.

By 1840 the Rev. Edward Jefferies lived at Glenthorne, which was known as 'The Old Vicarage'. He was curate from 1840 to 1862 and rector from 1863 to 1878, responsible for many alterations to St. Oswald's church. He married Martha Beatrice Dawson of Allan Bank, Mr. Dawson's younger daughter, having christened her twenty years earlier. After retirement from active work in 1878, Jefferies remained at Glenthorne until his death in 1893, aged 78. Martha Beatrice, his widow, and a leading representative of the Primrose League, spent the rest of her life at Glenthorne, and died in 1911 in her seventy-second year. Their grave is near Wordsworth's corner in Grasmere churchyard. Glenthorne was left to two nieces, Beatrice Isabella Mildred Twamley and Diana Edith Sophia Butt.

Linton Taylor, a Huddersfield carpet manufacturer and Quaker, bought Glenthorne and the Glenthorne part of the stables in 1923. On his death in 1961 he left these properties to the Westmorland and Yorkshire Quarterly meetings of the Religious Society of Friends, the Quakers. They agreed to rent the stables part of Bankside from the National Trust and converted the whole building into Bankside as it is now. The conservatory and additional space nearest to Grasmere village are more recent additions.

Bankside is now an annexe to Glenthorne. When the Wordsworth family lived at Allan Bank their cowshed was on the site of Bankside. There they kept one cow, for in those days there were no herds in a poor valley like Easedale: even a farmer who supplied milk would only have five or six cows. The part of Bankside nearest to Allan Bank was built in 1834. It housed three coaches and six horses, with further accommodation for a man who used the outside stone steps to reach his two rooms at the Glenthorne end. There were also two hay lofts, a corn room and a saddle room.

The Fieldside cottages now known as Fieldside 1, 2, and 3 were formerly the home of the Wilson family who owned the joinery business at Fieldside. The whole area comprising Glenside, these three cottages and the much newer adjacent housing estate is now called Fieldside. The cottages were built by John Wilson in 1858 using Helmstone from Easedale Quarry. The Wilson family continued to build many buildings in Grasmere at the turn of the century. The cottage block – that part of Glenside furthest from the road – was an office block and store room. The actual joinery was situated in the roadside buildings. At the height of its prosperity, forty men worked in the business, most of them outside on building work. Gunpowder for their quarrying work was stored in Fieldside 3 and two men were permanently employed in the rented Helm Crag quarry. As the business contracted the Wilsons' house was sold to make the three cottages as they are now. The Cottage Block was converted into a house and store room, the new office being built onto the joinery. In 1967 the property was bought and converted to provide extra accommodation for Glenthorne, but it has since reverted to private ownership.

21. Allan Bank

Allan Bank was one of the first 'big houses' in Grasmere, completed in 1808 for John Crump, a Liverpool attorney and merchant. At the time its classical style was totally alien to the Lake District. It was therefore not welcomed by everyone. William Wordsworth wrote to a friend:

> Woe to poor Grasmere for ever and ever! A wretched Creature, wretched in name and Nature, of the name of Crump, goaded on by his still more wretched Wife ... has at last begun to put his long impending threats in execution; and when you next enter the sweet paradise of Grasmere you will see staring you in the face upon that beautiful ridge that elbows out into the vale ... a temple of abomination, in which are to be enshrined Mr. and Mrs. Crump. Seriously this is a great vexation to us, as this House will stare you in the face from every part of the Vale, and entirely destroy its character of simplicity and seclusion. (*Letters*, I, 534)

Ironically William Wordsworth became the first tenant in 1808 and lived there with his family for three years until Mr. Crump needed it for his own use. Coleridge and De Quincey stayed at times during this period. Thomas Arnold was a tenant in 1832, whilst his new house Fox How was built. In 1834 the house was bought for £4100 by Thomas Dawson, a former barrister from Salford. He enlarged it with a new east wing and remodelled the interior, notably with a large new staircase. A Billiard Room was also built which looks very like a chapel. He also purchased other neighbouring land and buildings. Members of his family lived there until 1884 when it was leased to George Fothergill, Justice of the Peace, as a family home. In the late 1880s and early 1890s, future Liberal prime minister Herbert Henry Asquith spent holidays at Allan Bank with his family.

Canon Rawnsley, one of the founders of the National Trust, bought the property in 1915 and lived there from 1917 till his death in 1920. Eleanor, his second wife, continued in residence till her death in 1959 but handed the property over to the National Trust in 1951. In 1934 she added a loggia and french windows to the rear of the house.

The house was then let by the National Trust as home to three subsequent families or groups of tenants until a large electrical fire in 2011 which made it temporarily uninhabitable. Rather than refurbishing it to be let as a family home again, the National Trust chose to open it to the public, and have progressively restored the interior and the gardens, incorporating an art room in which visitors can try their hand at capturing the stunning views, and an important library of mountaineering literature on loan from the Mountain Heritage Trust.

Sarah Hutchinson, 'At Allan Bank' (1857)

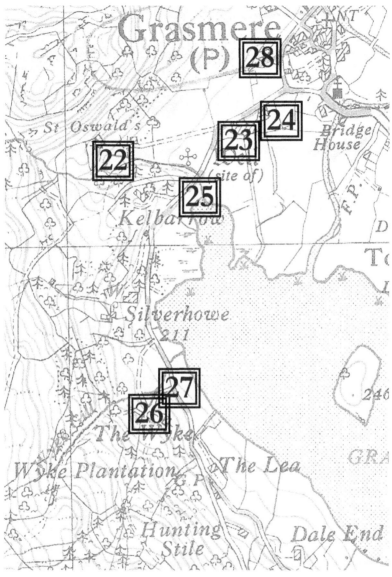

22. The Wray 　　　　　　25. Faeryland
23. Padmire 　　　　　　　26. The Wyke
　　and Pavement End 　27. Wyke Cottage
24. Grand at Grasmere 　28. Ryelands

22. The Wray

The Barony of Kendale records show that John de le Wra 'paid in goods £1' to the lord of the manor in 1332. This is probably referring to The Wray property. In 1375 William de le Wra paid 2s 8d yearly for two cottages and nine acres.

Parish records suggest the house was rebuilt in 1571. The property was redeveloped around 1844 and opened as St. Oswald's Hydropathic Establishment: a medical centre based on fashionable cold water treatments. The Establishment did not flourish. In 1960 the house was divided into two dwellings, but remains a Grade II listed building.

Extracts for the diary of William F. Sim who was a patient at St. Oswald's Hydropathic Establishment from October to December 1846 detail the treatments:

Charlotte M. Fletcher, 'The Wray' (1892)

Commenced operations by having a rubbing sheet applied. The Bathman came into my room in the morning with a sheet steeped in a pail of water and placing a large sponge bath for me to stand in, lifted in onto my shoulders and commenced rubbing me in good earnest, a process I joined as requested.

On looking at the Doctor's bill of Fare for the day was glad to find 'Large Douche 3 min.' This is the king of baths. The water here is supplied from the mountain torrent and falls in a perpendicular line 22 ft. the column being 2 to 3 inches thick. The force is tremendous and is sufficient to knock a man down who is not on his guard. The sensation after the first momentous shock is delicious, and makes one feel a man.

Packed and plunged as usual and walked with the Rev. Mr. Sheppard round the Easedale side of the valley to the turnpike and back.

The poet Wordsworth dined with us today with his son in law Mr Quillinan. Wordsworth's head is very well developed and bespeaks a large mind. His countenance is not pleasing, nor is his manner, being too self-satisfied even for an old man.

What sort of morning is it Robert, I said to the Bathman when he came to pack me. 'Hard frost, Sir' 'That's right' I said, and I jumped out of bed to prepare for the cold sheet. In about an hour and a half I took my plunge (biting cold) and sallied out with Miss. Dykes and Mr. Cookson to Red Bank returning by Hunters Stile.

Skated all over the Bay a feat rarely performed on Grasmere Lake in consequence of the great number of springs and the great depth of water. Glorious sport and every prospect of its lasting and that Rydal would bear tomorrow.

... I must ever regard the three months spent in the Hydropathic Establishment of St Oswald's as about the most happiest time taken for all in all I ever remember to have spent during my existence.

The hydropathic centre was situated at The Wray because the holy well of Grasmere, St. Oswald's Well, was in the field in front of the house. The famous Rushbearing ceremony traditionally began at the well before winding its way into the village. The well has been covered over since the late nineteenth century and is not now accessible to the public.

1910 Photograph

23. Padmire and Pavement End

In a 1664 church register, there is mention of a Pade-mr end. It is a Grade II listed building. Due to a pagan symbol at the back doorway of the adjacent cottage, the original farmhouse is thought to date as far back as the 16th Century. The dwelling was split to create two homes at an unknown date.

The marriage bands of John Green, read in 1788, refer to Padement End. This John Green had six sons and one daughter who died in infancy. The family are written of in Book 7 of Wordsworth's long poem *The Excursion*. Dorothy Wordsworth's journal records a November walk in 1801 when 'John Green's house looked pretty under Silver How'. Paintings of John and his wife Betty Fleming were made by William Bowness in 1848, and are currently held by the Wordsworth Trust. There was no particular road around the back of the lake till the mid-1800s and traffic passed through the farmyard to the fields between it and the lake.

The National Heritage List for England notes 'C19 additions and C20 alterations'. Built from coursed Lakeland stone and mainly cement rendered, there is a Westmorland slate roof covering, laid to diminishing courses. With three rendered chimney stacks, the listed building notice also notes a studded door and the irregular L-plan layout of the house.

From the mid-eighteenth Century until the early twentieth Century the occupant of Pavement End was likely a Green, as the Green family owned the property and worked the surrounding fields. As a result of this long association with the estate, this branch of the

Greens have connection to many other properties in the area, including those places now known as The Grand and The Wordsworth Hotel. An 1890 advert shows Pavement End as rentable for a summer, consisting then of 'two sitting rooms and five bedrooms, etc.' and with a telling nod to Victorian leisure pursuits, 'a Tennis Ground'. By the 1930s the farm was run by John and Mary Dixon.

The current owners have modernised the larger segment of the house. The Barn conversion to the rear is made up of two flats, converted in the mid 1960s.

Pavement End also described the broader area around the property. In the 1870s, the Grasmere Sports were held at the cricket field at Pavement End, which can still be identified by the tar topped stone wall. During the Sports, the wall was daubed with fresh tar to deter spectators leaping the wall, and thus gaining entry without paying through the gate.

24. Grand at Grasmere

Renamed The Grand in 2015, the building was previously known as the Gold Rill, Gold Rill House or Gold Rill Side, relating to the house's position beside a small beck. The original parts of the building were constructed in 1813, though it has since been much expanded.

For many years The Gold Rill was part of the estate of the Green family. It was the residence of the noted artist, photographer and publisher Thomas Andrew Green (known as Andrew) who traded with his brother James as Green Bros. (see **Ryelands** entry). The pair had developed their craft in St. Bees and documented vast swathes of Cumberland, Westmorland and Lancashire North of the Sands, publishing images of Lakeland which became famous worldwide.

Andrew also recorded village rainfall from 1888 and prepared a bathymetrical survey, measuring the depths of Grasmere Lake which he published in 1901, a year before his death in 1902.

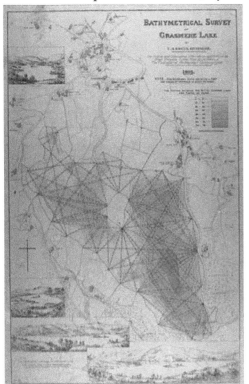

Andrew was the instigator of the Green's and Poor's charity which survives to this day. The charity was set up as part of the terms of Andrew's will: 'To relieve either generally or individually persons resident in the area of benefit who are in conditions of need, hardship or distress'. Andrew left a benefaction of £1,000, the annual interest of which the charity was to distribute among forty of the poorest inhabitants of the parish whom they judged most deserving.

The Raise Hospital for Infectious Diseases at Raise Cottage was also established as part of Thomas Andrew's will (see **Raise Cottage** entry). Some of this was administered by James but his swift death meant that much of the administration

Bathymetrical Survey of Grasmere Lake, 1901

passed to James' widow Eliza. The administration was made more complex by a court case, brought by Grasmere council to determine the extent of Andrew's gift to the public good.

Andrew's widow sold his photographic plates to Abrahams of Keswick, who reproduced many of his images on photographic postcards.

In 1915 the Gold Rill was placed in long-term let to frequent visitor, solicitor Gilbert Middleton of Leeds, until his death in 1922. Subsequently, Miss Emma Christiana Ascroft was resident at the Gold Rill. Miss Ascroft was daughter of Sir William Ascroft who had previously owned the Wyke. Miss Ascroft died in 1941 and a few years later, in 1948, the building became a hotel under the ownership of Mr. Frank Straw and Mrs. Edith Straw. The Straws ran the Gold Rill for many years, and oversaw many modernisations and extensions to the property.

When the Grasmere Players were founded in 1949, early meetings of the drama group were hosted here. The Players celebrated their 70th year in 2019.

The alteration of the Gold Rill into its Grand format reflects the changing taste and requirements of tourism in Grasmere.

Grasmere Publicity Association Advert, 1970s

25. Faeryland

Situated at the North-West of the lake, the boat landings at Faeryland have been a departure point for rowing boats since the late eighteenth century. The property is made up of a number of jetties onto the lake and a little building adjacent to the Red Bank Road.

It is recorded throughout the nineteenth-century as 'Well-foot boat landings', as the small bay of the lake that the landings face onto was historically known as 'Well-foot', being at the foot of St. Oswald's well (see **The Wray** entry). The bridge over the Wray Beck which feeds into the bay was known as 'welfoot bridge' as far back as the seventeenth century.

At the turn of the twentieth century the boat landing was run by George Fleming. One subsequent owner followed before the 1950s saw Joe Swalwell running the landings with his daughter Doris. Joe was said to have retired because the planning board reduced the level of the lake. This meant the landing stages were silted up. New landing stages were built at the same time as the weir was rebuilt at the bottom end of the lake.

In 1957, June and Derek Allonby rented the landings from the Mack family (who also owned Grasmere island – only on Miss Alison Mack's death in 2014 was the island bequeathed to the National Trust). The Allonbys began their seasonal business with only five boats, often

Etching of 'Grasmere From the Boat Pier', 1888

renting to fisherman and those on day trips. At this time, sheep grazed the island during the summer, having been boated across from the landings - six or eight sheep per boat.

In 1966, electricity and a water supply were installed, so June could start to supply tea, coffee, sandwiches and cakes. China tea sets and Twinings teas were served. From 1982 June ran the landings on her own but there are many who grew up in the village who recall spending their school holidays working for her at the boat landings.

June Allonby's stock of rowing boats grew, including some skiffs made from Thirlmere larch, and the increasingly cheaper Spruce skiffs. By 2000, June had sixteen rowing boats on the lake, eight fibreglass and eight wooden.

In 2000, Rick Martin, the present owner, took on the business and made substantial renovations to the small building, adding a sheltered wooden veranda and naming the tea garden Faeryland. The tea range expanded, whilst fibreglass boats are now rented most of the year, reflecting the increasingly year-round nature of tourism in the village.

Mr. Fleming at the Grasmere Boat Landing, 1912

26. The Wyke

The Wyke was originally built in 1801 by a George Cowperthwaite and doubled in size about 1853 by James Yates Greenwood, with the addition of two wings. However, what distinguishes The Wyke has nothing to do with its structure or architecture. It is the people who have lived in it, most notably the Ascroft family, three generations of whom occupied the house mainly as a summer residence from 1856 to 1947. The 1850s and 60s were decades when tourism was really starting to take off. The railway had come to Windermere and it was fashionable for prominent Lancashire families to own a summer residence in The Lake District.

William Ascroft headed one such family. He was a successful lawyer at Preston and used much of his resulting wealth to build houses for the poor in Preston as well as a school for disadvantaged children. He was also a champion of the rights of the poor and in 1906 he was knighted by King Edward for philanthropy.

James Greenwood, 'The Wyke' (1842)

The Ascrofts were also generous benefactors to St. Oswald's church in Grasmere and in recognition, one of its main stained glass windows is dedicated to Sir William's wife, Christiana, and the inscription can be seen there still. Nowadays it is often referred to as 'The Wyke Window'. Two similar windows are dedicated to the forbears of Sir Laurence Olivier.

However, above everything else, what really distinguishes the Ascrofts is that Sir William's son, William Fawell Ascroft, was also knighted some thirty years later for carrying on the same good works. It is believed that no other family in the history of England has had a father and son who were both knighted. Sir William Fawell was also a lawyer, and as one of the founder trustees of the The Friends Of The Lake District wrote its constitution.

Lady Eve Mary Ascroft (née Belk), watercolour of 'The Wyke' (1938)

27. Wyke Cottage

On 27th February 1614 John Hawkrig proudly carried his baby daughter home to 'The Wyke' from Grasmere church where, according to church records, she had just been Christened 'Helen'. And so begins the story of The Wyke estate. Hawkrig's cottage farmhouse, known as 'The Wyke' is believed to date from about forty years earlier, around 1575, and was at that time the only dwelling on the west side of the mere, from which came its name, because in the old Westmorland dialect, 'wyke' meant side or edge.

The Wyke kept its name until 1801 when a George Cowperthwaite bought the farm and built his gentlemen's residence up above the cottage on the fell side. This new house then became known as The Wyke and the original farmhouse, from then on, was known as Wyke Cottage.

Wyke Cottage is unusual today among old Westmorland farmhouses because it has never been rendered and whitewashed. It was built not with quarried stone, but using rounded boulders gathered from the surrounding land. Hawkrig almost certainly was the owner of this farm and not a tenant because historians note that the plank and muntin panelling, which divided the two ground floor rooms, has a carved edge detail which only an owner would have been able to afford. This confirms Hawkrig's status as being known as a Statesman.

The Hawkrig family's life in the early seventeenth century was harsh. Baby Helen would have been brought back from that February Christening to a cottage that was freezing cold. The living room, known as 'the down house,' had a flagstone floor which was deliberately set six inches lower than the entry threshold. This was so that the floor would retain and constrain a layer of hay which was strewn over the flags in Autumn, and then urinated upon. The urine caused the hay to ferment thereby generating a tiny, but much valued, background source of warmth. In the Spring the rotten hay was cleared away ready for the Summer giving rise to the expression 'Spring Cleaning.'

The main source of heat was from an open-hearth fire. Helen's parents would have lit the fire back in October and would have kept it alight continually until early April, but to gain much benefit Helen would have needed to be cradled very close to it. At that time the windows were only 'glazed' with waxed muslin and one of them, known as the 'fire window,' was always kept open to the elements to provide enough air to draw the smoke up into the bell shaped canopy above the fire.

Green Brothers Photograph, c. 1890

28. Ryelands

Ryelands was built in the 1850s. It has similarities to How Foot Lodge, another building of the period, such as the windows and ball-shaped finials on the roof. Inside the house there are three panels in the doors, an unusual feature that is mirrored in other houses in the village, such as Kellbarrow. Also there had been what oral history calls a Westmorland fireplace: where a fireplace was purposefully built in a window blocking the view from the outside (one suggested reason for this practice is it was a way to escape the window tax).

Early occupants were likely seasonal residents, with Dame Mary Euphemia White of Bassetlaw, Nottinghamshire, and Ann Kendall of Liverpool, amongst those who stayed here between 1860 and 1880. Peter Webb was a servant to the house living in the coachman's cottage for a large part of nearly 25 years. Peter's friends presented him with a china punch bowl and silver ladles on his departure from the village in 1884.

At the end of the nineteenth century, James Green lived at Ryelands with his wife Eliza. Their daughter Edith was born there in 1894. James and his brother Thomas Andrew, who lived at the Gold Rill, were well-known landscape photographers (see **Grand at Grasmere** entry). In the garden there is evidence of a track under the lawn leading towards the Gold Rill, connecting the houses. Together, they traded as Green Bros. Images from the Green Bros. were found in carriages and stations along the Furness railway, and on postcards. The pair famously photographed Ruskin outside Brantwood in 1885. James was also a prominent villager, both a member of the Local Board of Grasmere, and frequently presiding over meetings.

The house changed hands after James' premature death at 42. In 1909 it was sold to prominent Wordsworthian Edmund Lee. Lee had previously owned Dove Cottage and wrote a biography of Dorothy Wordsworth, *Dorothy Wordsworth: The Story of a Sister's Love* (1886) (see **Dove Cottage** entry). Lee's son, also called Edmund, was the secretary of London's Poetry Society and wrote a number of Lake District-set novels. One of those novels, *Helga Lloyd: A Romance of Grasmere* (1914) recounts the life of the village from spring to late autumn. After his parents and siblings died, Edmund Jr. lived at

Ryelands, in 1938 marrying Una Heaton Cooper, the sister of the artist William Heaton Cooper. Subsequent owners were William Alan Brooke in 1941; Phyllis Nicholson in 1945; Thomas Telford (formerly of Howe Foot Lodge) in 1948; Leonie (Lena) Parker in 1949; and the Le Corneaus in 1985. The present owners have had it since 1994.

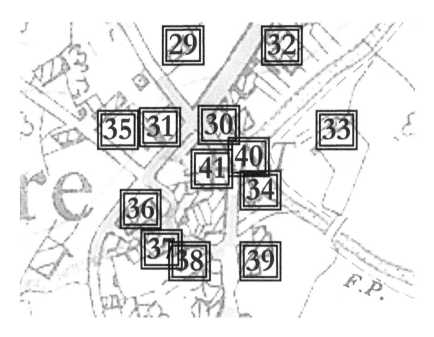

29. Dockwray Cottage
30. Broadgate House
31. Heaton Cooper
    Studio and Croft
32. Oak Bank Hotel
33. Rowan
34. Beck Allans

35. Wolvercote
36. The Inn at Grasmere
37. Heidi's
38. RAOB - The Buffs Club
39. The Wordsworth Hotel
40. Mountain Hi
41. Harley's Bistro

29. Dockwray Cottage

Dockwray Cottage is a Grade II listed white-washed cottage with attached barn in the centre of the village on Easedale road.

The exact date when Dockwray was built is unknown however similar vernacular buildings suggest that it was about 1650. It has the original nail studded wooden front door with simple wooden plank latch. Inside the plank and muntin partitioned front room is divided into living and sleeping quarters. Just by the open fire is a roughly-hewn alcove with wooden door which would have been used to store spices. Early maps do not refer to the cottage by name but Dockwray, Dockeray and Dockray were all local names. Dorothy Wordsworth referred in her Grasmere Journal of a visit on 28th May 1800 to Jenny Dockwray who lived at the cottage. She describes receiving a present of eggs and milk, and of enjoying the views from the garden. A few weeks later she wrote:

> 'In the morning walked up to the rocks above Jenny Dockerey's, sate a long time upon the grass, the prospect divinely beautiful. If I had three hundred pounds, I could afford to have a bad interest for my money, I would buy that estate and we would build a cottage to end our days in.'

Around 1900, the owners of Butharlyp How (now the Youth Hostel) bought Dockwray and installed a nurse there. Grasmere resident Richard Hardisty recalls that his aunt, born early 1900, had her tonsils removed by the nurse on the cottage kitchen table.

Irene Cooper Willis, a London barrister, literary scholar & author, along with her twin sister, Dr. Lynette Hemmant MRCS, LRCP, a gynaecologist, owned Dockwray Cottage from 1937 to 1953 and used it as a holiday home. Both Irene and Lynette were educated at Girton College, Cambridge between 1901 and 1904. Irene was executor for Florence Hardy, Thomas Hardy's wife, and trustee for Thomas Hardy's papers. Irene was also a prolific, well-respected writer of both fiction and non-fiction: she wrote biographies of the Brontës, Elizabeth Barrett Browning and Florence Nightingale. An ardent pacifist and feminist, Irene was a great admirer of Vernon Lee (aka Violet Paget) who is remembered for her supernatural fiction and work on aesthetics, art, music and travel. Also an engaged feminist, Vernon Lee always dressed 'à la garçonne', as did Irene on occasions, as reported by several villagers.

Dockwray Cottage was bought by Hermon Crook in 1953 when he retired from his architectural practice in Bolton (see **Dunnabeck** entry). After Hermon's death in 1969, Irene stayed on until shortly before her death in 1978. She was well-known in the village, and was always followed by a little flock of birds, attracted by the nuts and raisins distributed from her pocket as she pottered around.

30. Broadgate House

Noticeable today as the home of Sam Read Bookseller, in March 1865, Broadgate House is described in the *Westmorland Gazette* as a 'new and substantially-built premises'. It was likely built by the first person to let the building, Joseph Fleming Green. An advert outlines the shape of the building, 'comprising a good dwelling house and corner shop, the former containing three sitting and seven bed rooms. The shop has two large plate-glass windows, and from its central situation is well adapted for various branches of Business and may be taken either as a lock-up Shop or along with the House'. The two plate-glass windows are still prominent features of the shop today.

The first tenant was a photographer named James Sproat, who was one of a number of early photographers resident in Grasmere. Sproat, as R.J. Sproat, published *Stereographs of the English Lakes Scenery* in 1863. Mr. and Mrs. Sproat ran a boarding house, known as 'Sproat's Lodgings,' at the property between 1865 and 1879. Another early tenant of the main shop spaces from the 1870s was Thomas Bell, the chemist (whose name continues today in the Ambleside chemist).

From 1879, the tenancy shifted to Mr. Johnson Thompson. In August 1884 an advert in the *Lakes Herald* notes that Joseph Fleming Green was selling Broadgate House alongside 'four cottages, and Druggist's Shop adjoining'. This druggist would have been Thomas Bell. Additional property of Green's up for sale at this time included Beck Allans, Beck Steps, the Rothay Hotel, and even Langdale's Dungeon Ghyll New Hotel.

Mr. Johnson Thompson bought Broadgate House with a mortgage on it of £700. The next record relating to the house records the 1890 death of a houseguest: a 62-year old coachdriver by the name of John Hornby, known as 'Magpie', was buried in Grasmere churchyard.

In 1894, Johnson Thompson had fallen behind on mortgage payments, and allegedly upkeep, so the building was sold for £740 to local bookseller Samuel William Read. Read had been bookselling from Church Stile from 1887 (see **Church Stile** entry). Due to his lease at Church Stile, Read let Broadgate House to Thompson until 1895. Matters came to court when Thompson, a tailor and a renowned Helvellyn guide, would not vacate the property. Read, as Clerk to the Urban District Council, Clerk to the old Local Board, assistant overseer and a secretary for the Grasmere Sports, was judged to have the claim to possess Broadgate House. Accordingly, Sam and his wife Agnes (née Cowperthwaite), were trading as a bookshop and boarding house from 1896. One early worker at 'Mr Read's bookseller's shop', was a Mr. John G. Fothergill who went on to work at the Dungeon Ghyll hotel.

Sam Read sold books on the corner until his death in November 1919. Agnes Read kept the shop until her death in 1926, by which point their daughter Helen Read took over. The small bungalow on the Broadgate side of the building, sometimes referred to as Little Garth, was once an office for the Urban District Council. It subsequently became Helen Read's home.

Despite exploring a sale of the business in 1937, Helen Read kept Sam Read's until 1950, when the business was sold to Joyce Cockcroft. Joyce was known locally for her work in the theatre, and also wrote a play in 1950 specially for the Wordsworth Centenary entitled *The Wordsworths: a play in three acts*, presented by the Ambleside Players. Wesley Griffiths took on the shop in 1955. Griffiths left Leigh to settle in Grasmere, and bought The Wray. He had previously been involved with books through the Left Book Club in Leigh.

Margaret and Dan Hughes took over from the Griffiths' in 1969. Margaret had been a bookseller at Manchester's Haigh and Hochland. They ran the shop for 31 years. During Margaret's tenure, the floor was relaid and old bottles marked 'Bell' were discovered, dating back to Thomas Bell's tenancy. The present owner Elaine Nelson bought the shop from Margaret and Dan in 2000.

During the twentieth century the bookshop absorbed a small room which had operated as the Lancaster Banking Co. For a time this was a part of the children's books area of the bookshop but it is now the shop front of Lucia's takeaway. A parallel shop space on the other side of the front door was developed from a portion of the old boarding house. In the 1960s it housed Kate Greenwood's, which sold knitwear and tailored skirts. More recently, it has been Cunningham's outdoor clothing and in 2019 reopened as Lucia's Bakeshop, run by Elaine Nelson's daughter Lucia Nelson. There are still two flats above the shops.

31. Heaton Cooper Studio and Croft

The original Heaton Cooper Studio was a kit house imported from Norway by Alfred Heaton Cooper, and was first assembled in Coniston in 1904. It was later moved to a more profitable location in Ambleside, and now houses The Log House restaurant.

After his father Alfred's death, William Heaton Cooper took over management of the business. But when the family decided to move to Grasmere, William found himself trying to juggle his painting career alongside cycling to and from Ambleside to run the studio. He realised that for the family to survive financially, and that for his own painting career to be able to continue, the studio would have to move again.

In 1937, as he recounts in *Mountain Painter: An Autobiography* (1984) he resolved to build himself 'a good stone house, studio and gallery in the centre of Grasmere'. Undaunted by lack of funds, he set about producing a book, *The Hills of Lakeland*, illustrated with colour plates of his mountain paintings. Sales exceeded expectations, and the proceeds enabled William to purchase 'a small plot of land adjoining the village green', and to pay for the building work to start. As soon as the gallery was finished, he 'quickly hung up paintings on the walls and sold them in order to keep the men at work completing the next part of the building'. The 'next part' was a house for the family. This living accommodation, called 'The Croft', was designed to have the solidity of a vernacular Lakeland cottage combined with the simplicity of a modern 1930s house, and was attached to the studio and accessed via a door in the back of the gallery that led straight into the living space. This meant William's mother Mathilde could once more live on site and look after customers.

Following his marriage to the sculptor Ophelia Gordon Bell in 1940, The Croft became home to William's own growing family. A watercolour painted in 1947 depicts father, mother and three young children sitting out on the veranda, where three round slate-built columns support a flat roof that provides shelter from rain and sun.

With its clear, low profile and minimal signage, the studio stood in sharp contrast to the tall Victorian buildings that dominated the village centre. But the combination of white painted walls, dry stone pillars and oak doors gave it something of the style of the old lake district farmhouses – incorporating familiar local elements in a progressive format. The buildings were designed by the Australian architect Brian Bannantyne Lewis, who later became Professor of Architecture at the University of Melbourne. Bannantyne also designed the lakeside house 'Bowns Wood' near Brockhole.

The success of the business saw the studio expand, with the gallery extended northwards and a 'new studio' added in 1969. More extensions were added in the latter decades of the century.

In 2017, a previous storage area was turned into a dedicated space for changing exhibitions and a distinctive new café – designed by local architect Ben Cunliffe and named after William's mother, Mathilde – was built on to a previous exterior wall. The outside is brought inside, giving a high, atrium-like quality to the space. Surrounded with glass picture windows, there is a glorious view north to the high fells that William loved to paint.

William Heaton Cooper, Heaton Cooper Family at Croft, Grasmere (1947)

32. Oak Bank Hotel

On 2nd December 1863 the plot of land on which Oak Bank was built, commonly called 'Broadgate', was sold by William Pearson to Mr. Joseph Fleming Green.

The Oak Bank was built in 1872-3. The building then consisted of 'two sitting rooms and six bedrooms and a maids room' and horse stables, and was called Flemings Lodgings, Oak Bank. It is unclear if Joseph Fleming Green or John Fleming built the Oak Bank but in 1873 John Fleming (1826-1888), his wife Matilda and step-daughter Margaret owned and ran it. John was a house painter, employing two men, and Matilda ran the lodging house.

John Fleming passed away on 8th June 1888. He had a sad demise. That day, saying goodbye to a friend in the tap room of the Prince of Wales Hotel Grasmere around 4 pm, he seemingly walked down to the Lake, had a 'fit', fell in and drowned, aged only 62. Matilda moved to Ambleside with Margaret, and became a bookseller. Margaret's obituary in 1906 described their endeavour as a library.

Matilda sold Flemings Lodgings, Oak Bank, on 11th October 1888 to Mr. Samuel Abram Garside, (born 1st December 1860) who with his wife Emma (born in 1859) and their son Samuel Garside (born 1885). Samuel and his son Samuel were both painters and glaziers and plumbers. Samuel had the horse stable altered into his workshop: their painted sign can still be seen on a lintel. In 1900 Samuel also bought the adjoining land – 1,400 square yards – from Robert Wilson, together with lock up garages, and petrol pumps. It is notable that Samuel was an agent for the new invention of Gas Lighting in Grasmere.

Samuel Abram Garside passed the Oak Bank to his son Samuel on 31st December 1906. Son Samuel and his wife Violet Mary turned Oak Bank into a Hotel in 1920. On 23rd December 1937 Samuel died, and the following day his mother Emma also died, leaving widow Violet Mary Garside the Oak Bank.

Violet turned the plumber's workshop into a sweet shop. Violet lived and carried on the Private Hotel/Shop until 1956, when she sold it to Mr. Robert Mason Makinson and his wife Doris Mary Makinson for £5000, described then as 'a plot of 3,163 square yards together with Oak Bank, the shop adjoining, the lock up garages, office workshop and petrol pumps with tanks'. Violet bought Dunmail House, Grasmere, to retire into.

The Makinsons ran the hotel and property until 1959, when they sold it to Mr. James Mackintosh and his wife Elizabeth Emma Mackintosh. In 1969 James Mackintosh separated the businesses, selling the Garage known as the Oak Bank Filling Station to Mr. Fred Coleman. In January 1972 he sold the plot of land behind the garage to Sydney and Ada Taylor, who built their home there.

Douglas and Sybil Cameron bought the Oak Bank Hotel in January 1973. At this time, the hotel consisted of eleven bedrooms. Mr. and Mrs. Cameron put four of the bedrooms to en-suite and put central heating on the ground floor. The sweet shop had then been converted into staff accommodation. The holiday season then lasted from May until October. It has had two subsequent owners and sold again in 2019.

Oak Bank in 1965

33. Rowan

Rowan sits facing south in the vale of Grasmere, cloistered by natural charms and scenery. The River Rothay forms a natural boundary to the north and the west and grass fields encircle. Deeds dated 11th June 1970 describe a 'garden ground cottage and outbuildings' sold by the Rothay Hotel (now The Wordsworth Hotel), an early event in the hotel's demise (more fully described in Andrew Wilson's 1995 booklet *The History and Saving of the Rothay Hotel*).

In 1970, the plot contained a gardener's cottage with derelict structures. The new owner, a determined and progressive recently widowed woman, named the site 'Rowan' and began building.

The UK in the 1970s was to see severe inflation with economic and social upheaval. In 1975 inflation was an incredible 24.2% compared to 1.8% in 2019. 1970 was also the last year for the British pound in shillings and pence before decimalisation arrived in February 1971. From this era a number of items have been discovered under the floorboards, including a waxed paper bread wrapper. Branded Wonderloaf, and possibly from 1971, the wrapper was preserved in perfect condition, priced at 10p: the equivalent of £1.20 today. Another discovery, a copy of *The Sunday Times* is dated August 5th 1973, and is priced at 9p, now approximately £2.90. The paper informs that in 1973 the UK pound was worth US$2.50.

A home was created for the new owner and her visiting children

and grandchildren. Her further dream, a swimming pool, was enjoyed by everyone. Alongside this there was a garden room with kitchenette. The building also had a cream telephone: a luxury as only about half of British homes had one. A white-painted wall along the south and west featured large windows from a former car showroom.

In 1998, Rowan was bought by a new owner and the swimming pool became a sunken garden. At this point the white walls were also demolished. The stone wall on Rowan's east side (closest to the main road) and the outbuilding for the heating boiler at the southeast corner are both visible from the riverside path, from the north near  Broadgate Meadow and from the west near the Wordsworth Hotel.

Rowan could have been named The Old Vine House as it was built on the footprint of a Victorian glass vine house measuring 46ft x 20ft (14m x 6m), the grounds having been a kitchen garden for the Rothay Hotel. 'Grapes grown on the premises' declared Slater's Directory of 1884 as luxurious dessert grapes were needed for increasingly discerning guests.

The vine perished in 1947 in the extremely cold winter, and decay followed in the difficult years after the Second World War. Owners past recall spending many hours picking up broken glass, and the present owners continue to find shards. Rowan's walls now defend against the winds and its south face greets the sun. The site must have been carefully chosen long ago as Rowan was an island in Storm Desmond's floods in December 2015. It also has fell views at all compass points, with Helm Crag ('The Lion and the Lamb') to the North, Seat Sandal, Stone Arthur and Buttercrags to the East, Silver How to the West and Loughrigg to the South. Anyone can admire these views from the Permitted Riverside Footpath with benches facing south near Broadgate Meadow. Why not take Alfred Wainwright's advice in his guide to *The Central Fells* and 'tarry long over this exquisite picture of serenity and peace.' Although do remember these properties and their access lane are strictly private.

34. Beck Allans

Beck Allans was built in 1850. Much of the original structure remains. According to the deeds, it was built for four gentlemen: Mr. A. Nicholson of Plymouth, Mr. T. Green of Darlington, Mr. J.F. Green of Grasmere and Mr E. Tyson of Ambleside. It is assumed that the property to the north of Beck Allans now known as Holly Cottage was also built at this time as a stable block. The present entrance to Holly Cottage was original and provided a driveway to the property.

Initially William Green, a local landed proprietor, lived at Beck Allans,

and subsequently Henry Newsham, Esq. resided there. In 1871 it was lived in by James Coward, a joiner, and his wife Agnes (née Scott) and their family. Recorded with the family is a cousin, fifteen-year-old Jane Cowperthwaite, nurse, daughter of George Cowperthwaite and Elizabeth Dixon, and younger sister of Agnes Cowperthwaite (who marries Sam Read – see entry for **Broadgate House**).

The November 1876 Poor Rate Book records that the house is owned by a Mary Nicholson and occupied by Mr. Percy Ross Harrison.

The house served from 1875 to 1877 as a The Progressive College for the education of boys up to the age of 14 years, established by Harrison. Harrison was a well-known practising Spiritualist, and séances were regularly held at the college. The adjacent street is named College Street, which may relate to Harrison's school or to its subsequent use from 1890 as a Catholic College. In November 1877, after Harrison's college has closed, the Poor Rate Book records the house as owned and inhabited by J.F. Green, one of the original funders.

Miss Caroline Shipley lived at and owned Beck Allans from the late 1870s until her death in 1890. Caroline Shipley was responsible for building a temperance establishment (see entry on **Heidi's**). In 1886, she suggested Grasmere Local Board consider 'putting some guide-posts at the junctions of the roads in our village' having 'known some strangers to take the Easedale road in mistake for the road to Keswick'. These efforts led to the painted direction stone presently visible in the stone wall on Broadgate.

During the Great War, Beck Allans was used as a convalescent home for soldiers recovering from war wounds and shock.

Little is known between the wars until the Second World War when Beck Allans was a Guest House. One retired guest reported she would come here for her holidays. On Sundays she would go into the garden to pick vegetables for the Sunday lunch. An amazing lady, she was still visiting Beck Allans in 1989, travelling by taxi from Leeds!

In the 1970s the property, now owned by Mr. and Mrs. Yates, was converted into six holiday apartments. The adjacent Holly Cottage was the Yates' home. In 1988, Yates sold Beck Allans to Brian and Pat Taylor. Holly Cottage was sold separately and a wall was built to divide the two properties. The Taylors had plans drawn up for the construction of a six-bedroomed, six-bathroomed guest house. In January 1991 a two-storey wing to the rear of Beck Allans was demolished to make room for the new guest house which was then built on the cleared site, and which opened in July 1991. A great success, it was also hard work and needed two part-time staff to help run the business. In 2006, the Taylors retired, leasing out the guest house and converting a two-bedroomed holiday apartment into a comfortable one bedroomed retirement home.

35. Wolvercote

Built in the early 1960s, this was the last self-contained new build in the centre of Grasmere before the area became a Preservation Area.

This semi-detached property was built in the early 1960s by brothers J. B. and S. Fawthrop the owners of the adjacent Red Lion Hotel (now The Inn at Grasmere). An original plan to build two bachelor flats became two family houses. They were custom built with adjoining doors internally, both on the staircase and through a shared boiler room-cum-utility area. Each kitchen opened from this utility area into the houses, which were virtually a mirror image of each other. Trantunas was the name given to the left side of the property, Ventura the right. The name Trantunas was an anagram relevant to the owners.

The Fawthrop brothers purchased a quarter of an acre of land behind J.J. Hawkrigg's greengrocers shop (now Emma's Dell) for £300 from Peter Hawkrigg, who had previously sold a second parcel of land to build the Police House plus Office, now a 'holiday let' called The Old Police House. The piece of land had previously belonged to Under Howe Farm, becoming a Nursery Garden in the early 1900s. Finally the farm, slaughter-house and barns became holiday cottages after the death of Bob Borwick in 2005.

The Fawthrop families moved into their new homes in 1965. In 1973 extensions were built, forming the present building. Both houses acquired brand new large kitchens. Ventura also extended a

The building in 1965

bedroom above their kitchen. Two 22ft wide lounges became approximately 22ft square lounges, and Trantunas extended a bedroom above their lounge creating a break in the plain front of the whole house. The new portions of the property continued in the 1960s style using hard wood frames, fascias and including the decorative wooden 'dentals' beloved of the Yorkshire architect. Lake District slate was used on the roof and slate hangings. Two garages were also added. During the 1970s, the greengrocers became a café (first known as The Coffee Bean and then Miller Howe) and the vacant land beside the cafe became Nat West Bank. This was later absorbed into the cafe to form today's Emma's Dell.

The owners sold the Red Lion Hotel in 1988 and retired. Half the family eventually moved away. Ventura became Dumble Howe for approximately 5 years, and is now known as Green Hills. In 2014, Trantunas moved post codes and is now a small Lakeland Cottage. The 'new build' became Wolvercote when a retired DIY enthusiast and doctor of science moved in, bringing the interior into the 21st Century. He was there for about five years before returning south and rather sadly the house has now become a second home, though not yet a 'holiday cottage'.

Green Hills has also been much improved. The shared utility-room and doorway on the stairs have gone so the house is truly semi-detached, and remains a much loved home.

The building in 2000

36. The Inn at Grasmere

Known for most of its working life as The Red Lion Hotel, this prominent building is reputed to be the oldest hotel in Grasmere, dating back to approximately 1769. Then it also included two cottages and a Brewery containing two vats. The first landlord is recorded in Dorothy Wordsworth's journal as Mr. George Borwick . This would be the 'New Red Lion' as previously Newton's establishment at Church Stile had also been known as 'Red Lion'. During the period 1769 to the present day the Hotel has had approximately twenty-two landlords/owners.

Elleray's Red Lion Hotel, 1911

Jonathan Bell ran the Red Lion between 1820 and 1830. Anthony Wilson had it until 1831, and then later in the 1830s William and Ann Coats ran it. Whilst the Coats were tenants, Hartley Coleridge was known to have been in residence. Mid-century the building became synonymous with Isaac Usher. A second innkeeper by the name of Jonathan Bell took on the hotel from 1862 until 1865. Richard Hudson then rented the building from his brother-in-law Usher from 1865. Hudson expanded his interest in village property, also taking on the Rothay Hotel in 1874.

When Richard died in 1887, his wife Dinah took over the Red Lion, serving until 1898. Thirty-three years behind the bar meant 'Hudson's Red Lion' was a familiar advertising line in nineteenth century newspapers and guidebooks. Brief tenants from 1898-1899 were a Manchester couple, Mr. and Mrs. Henry Scholefield. Then from 1900 the Elleray family (formerly of The Swan) took over the Red Lion, and also owned Dale Lodge. Richard and Dinah Hudson's daughters, Dinah Elizabeth (1869-1934) and Florence (1873-1958) both married Elleray sons – John Elleray (1860-1909) and Robert Elleray (1872-1911) respectively – but it is another son, Frederick Elleray, who is proprietor of The Red Lion in 1911. Some further tenants include Samuel Bawden in 1913, Harold Lanhorn in 1935 and Mrs. Fielding in 1937.

The area which is now the dining room is the oldest part of the original building. It was once the old outside bar, the modern bar and toilets having been added in the 1890s. Opposite the car park the L shaped building now occupied by Cotswold was part of the Red Lion until 1988, and was originally built for stabling, used as the last staging post before Dunmail Raise. Originally stabling fourteen horses, a blacksmith's shop, forge and tackle room, above was a hay-loft which substituted for dances and gatherings for annual events such as Rushbearing celebrations. This was accessed by a large ramp. Over the years it was used as a garage, a newsagent, and a weaving shed complete with loom and gent's hairdresser. During 1976 the stables were converted into a Buttery Bar and a new Outside Bar named the Lamb Inn with staff quarters above.

Red Lion Square c. 1924

When the Red Lion was a coaching inn they employed a 'Boots' with the lovely name of Hoppie, who appears to have lived on through the centuries as a congenial smiling ghost. On many occasions Hoppie has been witnessed carrying out his nightly tasks. The Red Lion quickly established a reputation for hospitality and vittles. In 1792 Captain Joseph Budworth, author of the first published walking tour of the lakes, enthused over the overwhelming quality and service (see **Church Stile** entry). Towards the end of the last century Grasmere Sports committee banned the sale of alcohol on the sports field, thus giving the hotel an unexpected bonus.

The hotel has had many changes over the years. In 1966 twelve bedrooms with private bathrooms were added, one of the first hotels in the Lake District to do so. A large dining room was also added at this time. In 1967-8 a larger extension added seventeen more bedrooms with facilities, a new reception desk, cocktail bar, up-to-date kitchen extension and a lift. Unfortunately a major fire in 1974 destroyed an extensive area of the newly built alterations costing £150,000.

During the last few years the Hotel has undergone a number of further renovations, as well as being re-named The Inn and '1769 Bar & Restaurant'.

The Red Lion in 1974

37. Heidi's

A meeting was held in 1878 to form a 'Company, Limited, for the building of a Coffee Palace.' Many recognisable village figures came forward to support this endeavour, led by the chair at the meeting, J. Harward of the Hollens. It took three years before a coffee palace was built on the site of what is now Heidi's. In March 1881, the Grasmere Coffee Reading Rooms opened their doors, under the ownership of Miss Caroline Shipley (see **Beck Allans** entry). Initial plans mentioned the temperance movement, as the accommodation and reading rooms sought to provide desirable leisure space away from alcohol. Early adverts describe how 'the reading rooms are arranged to suit different classes and the library contains current and standard books'. Unlike the Reading Rooms or the Conservative Club, the Coffee Palace was less aligned with any one political group.

When Shipley died in 1890, the management of the property passed to Mrs. Sarah Bowness. Known as the Grasmere Temperance Hotel, Refreshment Rooms & Library, Bowness advertised the advantage of private apartments situated in the centre of the village. Sarah was married to John Bowness, a slate merchant, and was herself the niece of local builder Edward Wilson (who had known the Wordsworth family in his youth). In June 1907, American poet Harry Lyman

The Harwood Hotel in 1979

Koopman wrote to his friends recording his stay with Bowness: 'the house is comfortable and homelike, but the weather is that of Lapland in the days of Noah.'

Mr. Richard Thornborough and wife Lillie took over the running of the Temperance Hotel in 1911. Lillie was a daughter of local builder Joseph Casson Hodgson. In 1925, Mary Jane Whittam ran Whittam's Temperance Hotel from the building. Her daughter, also called Mary, ran it for a time with her husband Sea-Captain Lt-Commander George Thexton. George's father Thomas A. Thexton had had the Post Office at Crag House in the 1920s. The Thextons built and moved to Willow Bank next to the mini-roundabout at Town End.

In the 1960s the building was renamed the Harwood Private Hotel, most likely by the Harley family who departed in 1966. The Woods continued to use the name the Harwood Hotel, when they ran the establishment, until 1969. Ken Wood recalls being told that many years ago it had been known as 'the abode of love'! Extra bedrooms were added in the late 1960s. The frontage has also changed since the 1960s. Where there was once a balcony over a small garden with a wall round it and a privet hedge, these features have been removed and built over.

Three owners subsequent to the Woods have made their own mark on the building, the most significant being the development of a deli, or sandwich shop, separate to the main accommodation, which has itself changed names a few times. At one point this was known as Langman's Deli and now, like the accommodation, is known as Heidi's.

38. RAOB Club – The Buffs Club

Opened in 1906 as the Grasmere Constitutional Club, the building consisted of a billiard room 22ft by 20ft, and a reading room 18ft by 16ft, separated by a moveable wooden partition. Designed with lectures and socialising in mind, the building was closely linked with Grasmere's Conservative club. Original reports emphasised how unlike the Reading Rooms, the Constitutional Club would have a definite political affiliation. Although there was some discussion publically about the village supporting two clubs, Conservative backers felt that it was most likely that only the Reading Rooms would suffer!

The original trustees were Colonel Mair of White Moss, and George Murray Wilson of Dale End. The building was funded by subscription and cost over £600. Lord Lonsdale was only prevented from being at the building's opening by his own plentiful houseguests during 'shooting week'.

Early secretaries of the club were John W. Hodgson and Joseph Fleming. By the 1950s it was plainly known as the Grasmere Conservative Club, often playing host to party meetings and visits from then Conservative MP for Westmorland, William Fletcher-Vane. Records in 1997 note it was known as Grasmere Conservative and Unionist Club. By 2012 it was no longer a Conservative Club, but the building was still in public use for functions, craft fairs and as the regular meeting place of the Royal Antediluvian Order of Buffaloes, or the Buffs Club.

During the Saturday night of Storm Desmond's visit in December 2015, the building housed 28 travellers who had been rescued from a coach on Dunmail Raise by the Mountain Rescue. Peter Bailey, who has measured Grasmere rainfall for the Met office for nearly three decades, confirmed 261mm of rain fell in the 24-hour period of the storm on already saturated ground.

39. The Wordsworth Hotel

A farm was built here in 1630, on a site previously known as The Mosse. In 1853 Moss Head Farm was sold by John Green to the Earl of Cadogan who demolished it to make room for the building of Moss Head Lodge by Levi Hodgson. Unfortunately the Earl died in 1855 and the house reverted back to the Green family. In 1874 Joseph Fleming Green converted it to the Rothay Hotel, named after the adjacent river.

The 1876 Poor Rate Book record that it is owned by Joseph Fleming Green, but run by Richard Hudson (1830-1882) and his wife Dinah, formerly of The Red Lion (see entry for **Inn at Grasmere**). The 1881 census likewise records Richard Hudson as Hotel keeper and Farmer at The Rothay Hotel, though he died the following year. In 1887, the hotel passed to Edward Brown. Upon his retirement in 1894, one of his staff, Joe Cowperthwaite, of an old Grasmere family, took over. Family legend tells of Joe training a parrot to say inappropriate things to guests before delighting in apologizing on behalf of the parrot. At this time the hotel was one of the main coaching points on the north/south route through the Lakes.

Horses were changed there for the climb over Dunmail Raise, and fresh ones were available for the journey to Windermere Station and beyond. At one time 125 were stabled there. So great was the demand that when the London trams were electrified, the horses were sent

to Windermere by train. Many of them, bred for the tram service, knew only hay and nose-bag feeding and had never seen grass. It took them about two weeks to get used to it.

Activities for the guests included pony rides, tennis, boating and fishing. There was also a billiard room where the swimming pool is now. Woodrow Wilson stayed at the hotel in 1903 and 1908 prior to becoming the U.S. President in 1913. The business flourished under various owners during the inter-war years but after 1945 it gradually fell into decline and was sold at auction in 1970 (see **Rowan** entry).

Plans were drawn up for redevelopment as flats, shops and houses which led to many objections and the formation of the Grasmere Village Society. The Society raised public subscriptions, bought the property, then leased the hotel to Reg Gifford. He restored it to its former glory with the new name of the Wordsworth Hotel. The walls are built with the distinctive red stone from nearby Helm Crag Quarry. The multi-gabled slate roof is enhanced by ornate carved barge boards. It is now under new management and presents an attractive Victorian building in the centre of the village.

40. Mountain Hi

Edwin Tyson once used this building as a garage for his chauffeur and taxi business. Mountain Hi, an outdoor clothing firm, occupies it today. It still has the same folding doors at its front.

The English Lakes Perfumery used it as a showroom between 1965 and the late 1990s, having purchased the building from the Tyson family. The Perfumery was a business created by Sidney (Bill) Boots, a glove manufacturer from Southport, and industrial perfumer John Biden from Hale, Cheshire. Opening on Good Friday 1965 at 3pm as a mark of respect to the Methodist Church services of the day, the perfumery offered over 30 perfumes with Lakeland names e.g. Grasmere Rose, Keswick Gardenia and Langdale Lavender. Grasmere Rose was first offered for 10/6d or a half-guinea (52p) for a quarter of an ounce of organic perfume, equivalent to £9.25 today.

Sampling at the arcade 'bar' in the Showroom was encouraged for those who wanted to pop in each morning to try before they buy, by applying a glass dipstick onto wrists. Outlets covered the major part of South Lakeland, and also several department stores such as Kendal and Milne, Deansgate in Manchester and the Duty Free boutique at Manchester Airport.

Not only was concentrated perfume sold but also Eau de Toilette, aftershaves and bath oils, together with matching versions of private and exclusive blends for those who like his and hers toiletries.

Newspaper articles from the time inform us that staff was recruited locally, supplemented by family. Organic materials put the quality of the perfumes on par with French ones, encapsulating the essence of the Lake District.

An addition to the left was added as a toilet, for health and safety requirements, but the sanitary ware was never installed as the public toilets are just across the road!

Inside the Perfumery, 1979

41. Harley's Bistro

This building became Harley's Bistro in 2019. Prior to this, the building had been Grasmere's Methodist Chapel. The Wesleyan Methodist church was formed in the eighteenth century from religious societies founded by John Wesley and his preachers. It suffered much secession, but was the largest Nonconformist denomination in the nineteenth century.

Mr. Robert Hayton is integral to the early days of Grasmere Methodism. Hayton built a hut to serve tourists at Easedale Tarn (see **Easedale Refreshment Hut**), and was known in the village as a postman. Hayton's name is recorded in the original trust book of 1874. He was also the leader of the minute society in Grasmere and he collected £63 towards the cost of the new chapel mainly from visitors to the village. Once the initiative for a building had been taken, friends from all over the country made donations towards financing the project. Mr. Whelpton from London purchased the site for £42.12s and made a donation of £50 towards the cost of building.

Constructed in the Gothic style, the chapel was built to seat 250 people. The foundation stone was laid in June 1873 and the opening ceremony Thursday 4th June 1874. That service took place in the afternoon, conducted by Reverend Joshua Mason of Carlisle, Chairman of the District. He preached on transfiguration. Following the service a large gathering sat down to tea in the nearby drill hall (now no more). The total cost of the chapel was £700 and all but £100 of this had been paid at the end of the opening day. A presentation malachite clock was given to the architect, Mr. Rigg, who gave his services free.

The chapel was closed for evening services during the First World War until 1924.

The chapel was at the heart of the village, run by the congregation and hosted the children's playgroup. It had a strong Sunday school throughout the 1930s and its attendance was boosted in World War Two by the arrival of evacuated children from Newcastle-upon-Tyne and Bexley Heath, when many activities were arranged to keep the children occupied.

Due to lack of finance the church was forced to close in 2008 after 134 years of worship. Sold as a potential home, but unable to be converted due to planning and financial restrictions, it stood empty for a decade. In 2019 it re-opened its doors as a bistro.

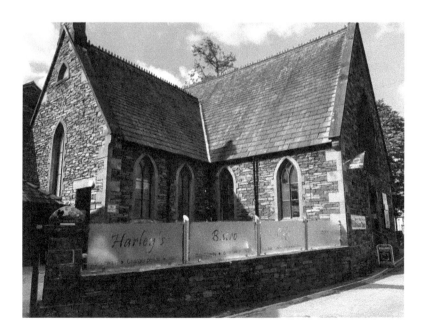

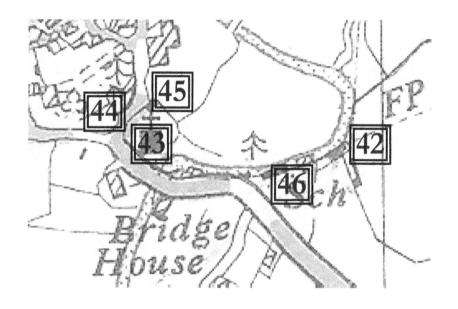

42. The Reading Rooms 45. Church Cottage
43. St. Oswald's Church 46. Grasmere School
44. Church Stile

42. The Reading Rooms

The Readings Rooms were erected in 1873, financed by Miss Elizabeth Agar of Silver Howe, for the working men of Grasmere, to enable them to socialise without the temptation of alcohol. A full sized billiard table and daily papers were provided, as were educational books which could be borrowed by members, including Shakespeare's plays. A gift of 250 books was made to the Reading Rooms in 1890 by the Hendersons who lived at the Hollens. Ongoing donations of money and furnishings from the Hendersons followed, at one point providing the Reading Rooms with an overmantel of oak, a new oak octagon table, twelve Windsor arm chairs and new flooring.

Whilst the Reading Rooms were meant to be non-political and designed to raise up the working men of the village, the Hendersons were strong Liberals and their interest in the Rooms was also seen as political.

A cottage was built adjoining the building to house the caretaker, whose job was to maintain and serve refreshments (tea and coffee). Early caretakers of the Reading Rooms were William and Mary Coates.

In Kelly's directory of 1914 the treasurer and honorary secretary was listed as William Fuller J.P. During World War Two, the building was used to school the evacuees, and after 1945 it became the school canteen, serving hot meals at lunch time. The Rooms have also hosted the Rushbearing Sports Monday afternoon teas.

'The Workman's Reading Room' is carved into the lintel of the doorway. The building became storage for a local joiner and resident until 2000, when the condition enforcing Temperance was overturned. Re-opening on 14th June 2003 as a village resident's social venue, the Reading Rooms' facilities now include live music, weekly bingo, billiards, snooker, pool, darts and dominoes. There are still educational books on display.

43. St. Oswald's Church

Situated by the banks of the river Rothay, Grasmere Church is an historic place of worship much loved by an estimated 140,000 visitors each year. Most famous now as the resting place of William Wordsworth, it has a long history which stretches back to the origins of the Christian Church in England. The church is dedicated to St. Oswald who died in 642AD. The present church is the fourth one on this site and the earliest parts of this building date from 1250. Remnants of previous buildings can be seen in the existing church, the most obvious being the stone head above the chancel. There are three external doors, the south door with the porch being the main door. The church did not have a west door under the tower due to the prevailing wet westerly weather. The small door by the altar rail is called the Lepers' door, or sometimes the Priest's door.

The Tower is built of un-hewn boulders taken from the riverbed. The walls are up to 4 feet thick. The clock was given to mark the Diamond Jubilee of Queen Victoria in 1897. Inside at the foot of the tower is the old Parish Chest from 1563 where parish records were kept. The font is fourteenth century. The nave windows are all post reformation.

St. Oswald's, c.1890

The memorial to Wordsworth (who is buried in the churchyard) located on the west wall of the nave was meant for Westminster Abbey but was purchased by friends of the sculptor Woolner and placed in the Church in 1851.

The north side of the church was added as a separate building in 1490 for the people of Langdale, however the gully between the two roofs collected snow and rainwater and was raised up in 1563 using stone from the curtain wall down the centre of the building where the arches were created.

The floor was raised and slated in the 1840s to cover the previous earthen floor which was covered in rushes every year from the lakeside. This tradition continues today as the annual Rushbearing Celebration, which takes place on the Saturday closest to St. Oswald's Day, which is 5th August.

44. Church Stile

This building, first recorded in 1638, was the Parish Guild House, and probably already an inn, known for some time as the King's Arms. The first recorded owner was Robert Harrison, who died in 1662. There was also a forge here and Edward Benson was blacksmith in the early eighteenth century, possibly shoeing travellers' horses. Cockfights were held in the grounds.

William and Dorothy Wordsworth probably spent a night here during their 1794 walk through the Lakes. William, his brother John and Coleridge stayed five days on their 1799 tour. There are several anecdotes about the inn-keeper of the period, Robert Newton. In 1810 Dorothy Wordsworth tells about his alterations to the house in a letter to a friend, Catherine Clarkson. During his long occupation Newton 'fenced unscrupulously' land next to the inn where the stocks stood – probably today's Storyteller's Garden. He also dammed a nearby beck to keep fish, and he is justly famous for the dinner he served to Joseph Budworth in the 1790s:

> Roast pike stuffed, a boiled fowl, veal cutlets and ham, beans and bacon, cabbage, pease and potatoes, anchovy sauce, parsley and butter, plain butter, butter and cheese, wheat bread and oatcake, and three cups of preserved gooseberries with a bowl of rich cream in the centre:--at 10d. a head.

Newton went on to open his new Red Lion about 1800 (see **The Inn at Grasmere** entry).

After Newton's death in 1836 Church Stile soon ceased to be an inn, but continued as a lodging house under various keepers. By the end of the century its use reflected the changing character of the village.

The 1876 Poor Rate Book records Church

Stile as owned and lived in by Ann Wilson. In 1881 and 1911 censuses Mary Green Wilson (b. 1840) is living here, with her occupation recorded as either 'Private school teacher' or 'Living from houses and land.' The Wilsons are assumed to be the Ann Wilson and her daughter Mary Green Wilson previously recorded at Goody Bridge (see **Goody Bridge** entry).

In 1884 Samuel Read, the bookseller, who held many responsible village posts, became the tenant (see **Broadgate House** entry). When Read left in 1894, Robert Hayes moved in to establish his gardening and nursery business and continued to live here till his death in 1947. Miss M. Parsons was the next resident when she opened her haberdashery shop which continued till 1968.

In that year, to avert the threat of a block of flats being built on the site, fourteen far-sighted and generous residents bought the property and gave it to the National Trust. Most of the ground floor is now occupied by the National Trust shop, and the rest of the building is a family home. The studio at the northern end was used by artist E. Greig Hall for over 30 years and latterly by Taffy Thomas, the storytelling laureate, as his Storytelling Centre. The building displays several features of the vernacular architecture, such as the lime rendered, two feet thick walls built from locally gathered and quarried slate. The much-altered interior has some slate floors and typical low ceilings. It is a Grade II listed building.

Sam Read Bookseller in Church Stile, c.1890

45. Church Cottage

Now known worldwide as The Grasmere Gingerbread Shop, the home of unique Grasmere Gingerbread®, Church Cottage is one of the most iconic single storey stone dwellings in the UK. It is entirely synonymous with the life and times of the Victorian cook and businesswoman Sarah Nelson.

Church Cottage was built to be Grasmere village's school and paid for by public subscription. Former schoolmaster William Fuller dated the building to the time of Reverend John Ambrose in 1660. This was long before an 1870 Act of Parliament made education compulsory for children aged five to ten. The building originally offered local boys basic schooling, provided their parents could afford a fee. Between 1687 and 1713 the Reverend Mr. Thomas Knott was the 'Ludimagister et clericus Grasmeriensis' (Schoolmaster and Clerk). Before the nineteenth century few schools for the masses existed, and those that did were run by church authorities and prioritised religious education. Knott's successor was Reverend William Johnson, who along with the poet William Wordsworth practised the Madras method at the school, in which older children instructed younger children. Johnson was so successful in this that he was headhunted

by William Bell, who employed him to teach at the new National Society School in London after seeing his teaching in Grasmere. Later schoolmasters were laymen, and included William Baldry, Edward Button and William Fuller (see **Grasmere School** entry).

The school was converted into a dwelling – initially called Lych Gate Cottage and latterly Church Cottage – in the mid-nineteenth century after a larger school was completed nearby. In 1854 – the year that Sarah Nelson invented Grasmere Gingerbread – she moved in with her husband Wilfred and two daughters Mary Ann and Dinah.

Adjacent to the St Oswald's Churchyard lych-gate, its location was convenient for Sarah's husband who worked as a gravedigger. Wilfred also worked for local builder Levi Hodgson, and was a great fisherman, making fishing rods and dressing flies for a host of fishermen. In her kitchen Sarah mixed and baked Grasmere Gingerbread before selling it to passers-by from a tree stump outside her front door. In keeping with the building's educational past, Sarah created Grasmere Gingerbread letters, covered them in thin horn, and taught local children the alphabet.

Sarah was identified in the 1871 census as 'Baker and Confectioner of Church Cottage, Grasmere,' becoming known for her 'spice shop.' A picture of her outside the house was incorporated into the original 'None Genuine Without Trademark' logo that is used on Grasmere Gingerbread packaging today. After the tragic deaths of her daughters from tuberculosis in 1869 and 1870, and the passing of her husband in 1880, Sarah continued to live and work at Church Cottage until her death from 'exhaustion' in 1904. Two great nieces took over the business following Sarah's death.

Today, the Grasmere Gingerbread Shop welcomes tourists from all over the world and Gingerbread is still made fresh there 362 days a year. You can still see Sarah's storage pantry with wooden shelves, sturdy stone sills and curious nooks and crannies that evoke her past.

46. Grasmere School

From its humble beginnings as a small single-roomed school in the corner of the churchyard, built by public subscription 1660 (see **Church Cottage** entry), Grasmere School was relocated to a new building on its current site on Stock Lane in 1854. Successive expansion took place to accommodate an infant school in 1862, and a further enlargement occurred again in 1879. Mr. William Fuller, headmaster of Grasmere School for some forty-odd years in the late nineteenth century, lived on site in the adjacent School House, with his wife and seven children. Fuller's log-books, a pre-requisite of all Victorian schoolmasters, are a vibrant source of history of Grasmere School. The log-books present a fascinating glimpse into a building steeped in history: mention of extreme weather, population movements, school inspectors and spirited children offer reassurance that little has changed across the school's 165 year history.

Major national and world events did not escape this relatively remote rural school population, with holidays being granted for Queen Victoria's Diamond Jubilee and for military 'successes' such as those at Ladysmith and Mafeking during the Second Boer War (in March and May of 1900, respectively). Grasmere pupils bore witness to landmark occasions, such as technical innovations of the Industrial Revolution, watching early motorcars being driven through the village.

The building suffered structural problems due to flooding (1882) and storm damage (1892) which actually took off part of the roof, and the classrooms appeared to be incessantly draughty. There was much concern about over-crowding, with record numbers of 'scholars' being listed, including 110 pupils in the juniors alone, which brought additional logistical problems to the building such as where to situate a new urinal block for the boys. Despite children being packed in to the rafters, there was pressure to retain pupil numbers, due to competition with a fledgling dance school that emerged in the village and absenteeism for a myriad number of reasons: poor weather conditions, children staying on their home farms to help with the harvest, taking employment illegally, or pupils simply playing truant (especially during the popular Grasmere sports day) and because of illness, particularly measles, influenza and whooping cough epidemics.

There was an increase (on many occasions) in rough play which required discipline amongst the children on days when football was banned, and only the most unruly pupils, (or conversely, children who merited particular praise) being mentioned specifically by name.

Grasmere School has also proved important in terms of population movement. The school played host to a number of children from industrial cities like Manchester whilst their fathers laboured on the Thirlmere Aqueduct. It also provided a safe haven for an influx of more than forty pupils from Kent seeking refuge from Nazi bombing during the Second World War.

More could have been said on the architectural history, but it is the people within the walls that have always made this building what it is. Now operating as Grasmere C of E (VA) Primary School, the aforementioned headmaster's home has also been utilised as a teaching space in much more recent history.

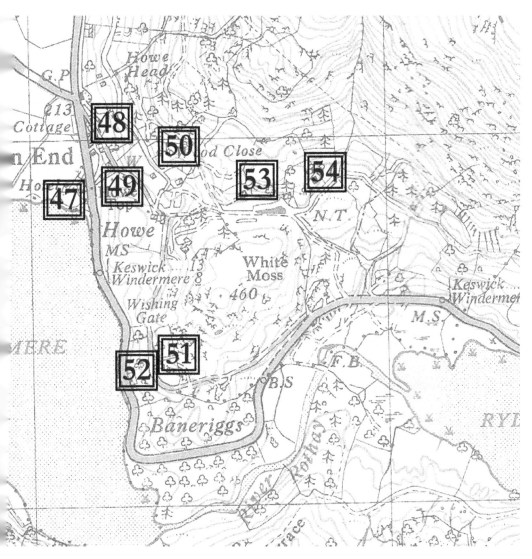

47. The Daffodil Hotel
48. Dove Cottage
49. How Top Farm
50. Wood Close
51. Ladywood
52. Banerigg Guest House
53. Heugh Folds
54. Dunnabeck

47. The Daffodil Hotel

The Daffodil Hotel was first known as The Browns Lake Hotel when it was built at the northern end of Grasmere lake in 1855. The hotel was built for the owner, Edward Brown, by 46-year-old Levi Hodgson. Levi was listed in the 1851 census as a farmer of sixty acres and a builder employing twenty-one men, living at Town End with his wife Elizabeth, ten daughters and his youngest child Aaron. Levi was responsible for building other impressive buildings in Grasmere including Cragside (see entries for **Wood Close** and **The Hollens**).

Brown changed the name of the hotel to the Prince of Wales Lake Hotel after a royal visit by the Prince of Wales in 1857. An 1866 guide printed by the hotel recalls the visit and describes the business as under the patronage of The Prince of Wales and Prince Arthur. When Prince Arthur visited in 1863 'two oak trees were planted on Grasmere island, in honour of the marriage of his brother the Prince of Wales'.

Edward Brown died in 1865 and the running of the hotel was passed onto his son, also named Edward. Sadly, the younger Edward

The Prince of Wales, 1965

died in 1884 at the age of 38. The hotel continued under the management of his wife. The Prince of Wales was unique amongst the village's hotels, in that it had its own gas works and lit the hotel from these. The gasworks were at the edge of the Howe above Howe Foot Lodge.

In 1911, Joe Cowperthwaite was the proprietor of the Prince of Wales, along with the Rothay Hotel in Grasmere and the New Dungeon Ghyll Hotel at Langdale. Relatives of Cowperthwaite, the Scott family, ran the Prince of Wales from the 1920s. The Scott family also ran Scott's (Grasmere) Motors, to transport people back and forth to the railway station at Windermere.

The name of The Prince of Wales remained until fairly recent times when it had brief changes to the Thistle Grasmere, and then The Waterside Hotel.

The driving force behind the hotel's recent redevelopment was the late Tom Harwood, who had been a builder and hotelier in the area for over 40 years. Tom died suddenly before the foundations were laid, but his family pressed ahead with his plans and two years after his death the hotel was finally reopened. After extensive rebuilding and renovation The Daffodil Hotel opened in July 2012.

The hotel produced its own local guidebook in 1866

133

48. Dove Cottage

Dove Cottage is best known as the home of the poet William Wordsworth, his sister Dorothy, his wife Mary and their children. Wordsworth rented the cottage from John Benson of Dale End from 1799-1808. Prior to this the cottage had been an inn, The Dove, or Dove and Olive Bough.

Visitors to the Wordsworths' home included Samuel Taylor Coleridge, Sir Walter Scott, and Thomas De Quincey. De Quincey rented it himself from 1809-1835, living in it only intermittently after 1820, whilst continuing to use it as a library for his infamously vast book collection. In *Recollections of the Lakes and the Lake Poets*, De Quincey described his 'beloved' cottage, whose 'associations with Wordsworth crowned it ... with historical dignity.'

After the De Quinceys, the cottage, still under the ownership of the Benson family, had various tenants, including Letitia Luff (from 1837-1841), a shoe-maker called Gawin Mackereth and his family (from 1841), and the Wordsworths' friend Elizabeth Cookson and her daughters (1843-1846).

The house also had frequent boarders seeking to follow in Wordsworth's footsteps. In 1859 one such lodger published an account detailing how:

'The pretty little cottage in which I have a room was some fifty years ago occupied by William Wordsworth, and the practical labour of his hands is to be seen in the ascending series of rough blocks of slate which he laid in the turfy mountain.'

In the 1860s it was run as a lodging house by John and Jane Dixon under the name 'Dixon's Lodgings: Wordsworth's Cottage', making the most of the growing numbers of literary tourists. Through the 1870s and 80s it was home to a series of local working families, who also took in boarders, many of whom wrote accounts of their Wordsworthian holidays.

Amos Green, 'Dove Cottage' (1800)

Its last private owner was Edmund Lee, a solicitor and Wordsworth enthusiast from Bradford, who wrote the first biography of Dorothy Wordsworth (published in 1886). Lee bought the cottage in June 1888 to preserve its Wordsworthian heritage, and would later describe it as one of his 'most treasured possessions'. Lee let the cottage to Charles Walmsley, who worked on the Thirlmere reservoir, and his family. It seems Walmsley shared Lee's passion, as he named his daughter Dorothy Wordsworth Walmsley.

In 1890 Lee was persuaded to sell the cottage after Stopford Augustus Brooke - Queen Victoria's chaplain and dedicated Wordsworthian - circulated a pamphlet asking for subscriptions to fund the purchase 'for the nation and for posterity'. Lee continued to live in Grasmere, at Ryelands, until his death in 1931. (see **Ryelands** Entry)

It is a great irony that one of the first acts of the Dove Cottage Trust in 1891 was to evict a Dorothy Wordsworth from Dove Cottage.

Dove Cottage is the third oldest writer's house museum in England, after the Shakespeare Birthplace Trust, and Milton's Cottage. It has now been a museum for longer than it was ever a home, and represents a fascinating history of changing ideas about what museums are and can be. It is preserved by the Wordsworth Trust as 'the inspirational home of William Wordsworth', but its history has much more to offer than that alone.

49. How Top Farm

How Top Farm was built around 1611 as one of Grasmere's high farms to escape the boggy bottom of the valley floor. The ground at How Top is very like the lake floor: if you dig four feet down through sand, soil and shiller you will find tree roots. Although on the outskirts of the hamlet of Town End, the farm is actually in the parish of Rydal and Loughrigg.

How Top Farm has a fine example of a fifteenth-century bank barn in its grounds noted for its entrances on two separate levels which both meet the road. This is one of a few remaining bank barns in South Lakeland, which would once have been a common sight across the region.

How Top's existence was noted in Dorothy Wordsworth's Grasmere journals, when the sitting tenant was John Dawson. Another notable tenant was Levi Hodgson (born 1809). Hodgson moved from Patterdale to the area to find work, married and had 11 children at How Top. The censuses of 1841-71 show a man building his reputation as a farmer and builder. In 1855 Hodgson was a stone mason; in 1861 a master Waller; in 1871 a builder and in 1881 he had retired to How Top. Hodgson built nearly all new houses of the Victorian tourist boom in Grasmere, or what William Fuller, and many villagers termed the 'intrusion'. Hodgson had a large company of workmen who would troop into Grasmere over White Moss every day from Ambleside.

From 1891 How Foot Farm House was occupied by farm bailiff Daniel Jenkinson, aged 70 at that time, and his family. Jenkinson was bailiff to Mrs. Elizabeth J. Brown, then owner of the Prince of Wales Lake Hotel.

Even though Levi Hodgson never owned How Top, the 1901 census refers to the property as Levi's Hodgson farm, occupied by a Scottish gardener Albert Smith and his family. In 1911, a William Williamson and family occupy the house.

Oral history research documents that the Parker family were tenants between 1929-1932. During World War Two the farm was still used by the Prince of Wales hotel and supplied the hotel and village with milk. At this time Mr. and Mrs. Jim Knowles were tenants.

In 1967 David and Judy Thompson, who worked for Jim Knowles, took over the farm. On their retirement they sold it to a couple from Lancashire who 'renovated' the Grade II listed building, though it remained mostly empty for the large part of a decade. In 2019, How Top Farm sold again, with seven acres of land.

Charlotte M. Fletcher, 'How Top, Grasmere' (1896)

Mrs. Knowles feeding the geese

50. Wood Close

Access to the Lake District was greatly improved when the railway line was extended to Windermere in April 1847. Large Country Houses were built by industrialists from Lancashire and Cheshire; numerous examples can be seen in the Windermere, Ambleside and Grasmere area.

Transport from the railhead at Windermere to Grasmere would have been by horse coach along lakeside roads until the advent of cars, fifty years later.

The 'new' road to Grasmere along the Lakeside was opened in the late 1820s, replacing the original route via Town End, at the bottom of How Head Lane.

Wood Close was built by Levi Hodgson who lived at the farm opposite the duck pond (see **How Top** entry). The land was released for building in 1848 and the house was built between 1858 and 1860 in the traditional style of Victorian houses in this area. Hodgson also built Cragside, Woodland Crag, and the Prince of Wales Hotel. Wood Close was built for Hodgson's own family and two of his daughters ran it as a boarding house until it was sold to Dr. Halton of Liverpool in 1869. Halton owned the property until 1916, when it passed to Sarah Roberts. From 1920 until 1935, Mary Brooke owned the house, with it then passing to Reverend Henry Symonds until 1944. Subsequent tenants were Ethel Coller, Bertha Hewitt (Powell), Frank Brotherton, Ethel Harris and Edward Cole.

In 1962, the house was converted to two apartments and a maisonette. Residences called White Moss and Langdale were created in 1967, alongside a conversion of garage and other rooms into Pavey Ark and The Old Coach House. In 1975 apartments named Silver Howe and Helm Crag were built; in 1990 Fairfield was built. More changes in 1994 saw the front of the house split into Wetherlam and Buckrheddan (renamed Rydal in 1999). In 2004, Wetherlam and Rydal were converted back into one unit, Wetherlam.

The main entrance to Wood Close was through the doorway of Wetherlam with a staircase to the upper floors. The kitchen was located in White Moss, hence the water pump near its door. Rambler's Roost (formerly Pavey Ark) was the horse and coach stable with the Old

Coach House being the coachman's residence. The water supply was from ponds and streams on the fellside until 1885 when the aqueduct from Thirlmere to Manchester was built. The aqueduct runs underground about 400 yards above Wood Close and a branch pipe supplied water until mains water was introduced.

The original garden would not have had rhododendrons, which were introduced to the UK at a later date. The Sequoia tree must have been imported from the USA and now around 140 years later has grown to over 120 foot in height. The beech tree alongside the drive must also be of a similar age. A tennis court was built below the Sequoia tree and a kitchen garden on the other side of a small stream where the remains of a heated greenhouse can still be seen. At the bottom of the garden is a very old Witch Hazel, best seen in January and February when the scented yellow flowers are out.

Prior to Wood Close Management Company Ltd. purchasing the property in 1993 there were twelve previous owners.

51. Ladywood

In 1898 there was the idea of development of a group of houses in the area towards White Moss. Only two were ever built, Banerigg (see **Banerigg Guest House** entry) and Ladywood.

Ernest de Selincourt persuaded the Flemings of Rydal Hall to sell some of the woodland called Lady Wood so he could build a home where his family could have holidays while he researched William Wordsworth's life and work. This house has been the home of the same family for four generations. The other half of Lady Wood remains a natural beech wood.

Ladywood was built in 1904, with a room at the top designed to be Ernest de Selincourt's study. He had four young children so he later decided it would be better to have a separate building as a study. In 1914 this was completed. The family story is that this small building cost the same amount to build ten years later as the main house in 1904, partly due to inflation and partly because space for it had to be created by blasting into the rock beside the house.

In the 1920s and 30s the house was the centre for this family's life, with many holidays including walking and cycling trips around the area. One of his children, Oliver, used the room at the top of house again as his study bedroom during summer holidays.

By 1939, Ernest de Selincourt was widowed and living at Ladywood. It is likely that he had a couple living with him, to do the gardening

and housework. Some of his grandchildren were moved from the south to be educated as weekly boarders at Keswick School, so Ladywood became their home for weekends and holidays. They travelled between Keswick and Grasmere either by bus or by cycle. The routine while his grandchildren were there included an hour's gardening before lunch together as a break from Ernest's study of Wordsworth.

World War Two was a busy time for the house, with the Spencer family being put up when the Royal College of Art was evacuated to the Lake District. Gilbert and Ursula moved to Ladywood with their daughter Gillian. Gilbert Spencer drew and painted the family and garden while at Ladywood. It is likely that the Spencer family helped with the running of the house and garden while staying there so there was no need for other help. Paintings of the garden by Gilbert Spencer show the layout has remained similar.

Ernest de Selincourt died in 1943 and the house reverted to being used as a holiday home, with a local couple caring for the house and garden while it was empty. In 1963, Ernest's daughter Mary and her husband Charles retired there. One photo shows them walking on White Moss with many fewer trees and other images show the views were clearer.

Two more generations have passed and, with each change, the house and garden are adapted to current needs but many things remain undisturbed.

Ladywood in 1965

52. Banerigg Guest House

In 1898 plans were drawn to build twenty-five properties on the woodland known as Lady Wood and Baneriggs, but only two properties were actually built; Banerigg House and Ladywood.

'Baneriggs' House was built in 1900 by the le Fleming family of Rydal Hall. In September of that year the house was leased to a Mrs. Elizabeth Grasse, wife of John Grasse, for £4.00 per annum. Elizabeth had five children, a son and then four daughters. In the 1901 census Elizabeth was living at 'Baneriggs' with her husband John, a gamekeeper, two of their five children, Mary and Elizabeth Maria (widow) and Elizabeth Maria's four-year-old son. In 1907 Elizabeth bought the house from the le Flemings for £173.00.

Postcard, c. 1925

By the 1911 census Elizabeth Grasse, now herself a widow was living at Banerigg with her youngest daughter Lillie and a lodger. Elizabeth's older girls Mary and Elizabeth Maria had moved to Blackpool. Banerigg was listed as a Boarding House. Lillie was soon to become the wife of a chauffeur Herbert F. Robertson who was lodging at West View, Grasmere, at that time.

Elizabeth died in 1916. She left the house in trust to her four daughters. Firstly to the eldest daughter Mary to 'use and enjoy during her life and at death the house was to pass to her next surviving sister and so on in turn. Mary died in 1946 and following the terms of the trust Banerigg passed to Elizabeth Grasse's next surviving daughter Emma, now Emma Lenzini. Two years later in 1948 Emma sold her share of the house to her brother in law Herbert F. Robertson (Lillie's husband) for £2000. He sold it five months later for £6500. For the years between 1916 and 1948 it appears that Banerigg was a family holiday home, not a permanent residence as all the siblings lived in Lancashire or America.

The house changed hands frequently from then until 1979 when the current owners moved into the property, but Banerigg has been used continuously as a guest house since 1948.

In 1967 Banerigg was bought by a London barrister Mrs. Holland and leased to a widow Mrs. Lilian Lane. Mrs. Holland writes that, 'surprisingly in the summer of 1967 there was a drought in the Lake District and my water supply ran dry. I had to make arrangements for a water supply for Banerigg and one of them was to fetch water from the lake to supply the house lavatories. It was as a result of this crisis I had a main supply of water brought to the house at considerable expense in 1968.'

In 1981 an extension added a larger kitchen and owners' accommodation. A further extension in 1994 added four en-suite bedrooms to meet changing customer demand.

Banerigg has seen many visitors over the years, many following in the footsteps of Wordsworth. Modern-day authors still seek inspiration from this area and books about Wordsworth, Dr. Who and even a murder mystery have been penned by guests of Banerigg.

Grasmere Publicity Association, 1967

53. Heugh Folds

Heugh Folds was built by Anna Deborah Richardson, a member of a prominent Quaker family from Newcastle upon Tyne. Anna was an early feminist, being a member of the English 'women's movement', and helped her friend Emily Davis to establish the first higher education college for women that became Girton College, Cambridge. Heugh Folds was intended as a place where Anna could live independently, entertaining her like-minded, intellectual female friends.

The land was purchased from Levi Hodgson. He constructed the house for Anna, to her own design, which reflected her Quaker faith and the Gothic Revival architectural style of the time. Heugh Folds was completed in early 1864 and Anna decided that its motto should be 'Ubi charitas ibi claritas', meaning where there is love there is clearness.

In 1867 Anna also built the three neighbouring Tarn Cottages as comfortable dwellings for local workers to live in. Sadly Anna suffered from poor health and died at Heugh Folds in 1872 at the age of forty. Following her funeral one of the Grasmere boatmen commented 'she was the best lady that ever lived in this valley'.

In her will Anna left Heugh Folds to her younger sister Caroline who owned the house for over forty years. In 1889 Caroline built the water fountain at Town End in memory of Wordsworth, having it inscribed with her own initials and those of her sister Anna. Edwin Heathcote, in a 2018 *Financial Times* article, describes it as:

> perhaps the most complete item of English street furniture: it combines a trough (with a little lower-level extension for dogs), a Romanesque niche for the fountain itself and a stone bench on the other side. Being good to animals, a drink, fake medieval nostalgia and a nice sit-down. The perfect English day out embodied in one piece of public design.

In 1921 Heugh Folds was acquired by Anna and Caroline's nephew, Charles Hesterman Merz. Charles, an electrical engineer, was a major figure in the development of electricity generating across the world and invented the National Grid. He made several improvements to the house and acquired much of the surrounding land, including Alcock Tarn and Brackenfell, which he opened to the public in association with the National Trust.

Charles and his two children were killed in an air raid in London in 1940 and ownership of Heugh Folds briefly passed to his younger brother Norbert before coming into the hands of his sister Teresa Merz, OBE.

Teresa was a magistrate, a suffragist and a lifelong voluntary social worker, working with war victims in the Great War and playing an important role in the development of social services on Tyneside during the early twentieth century. In 1939 a nursery for illegitimate babies and toddlers that Teresa had established in Newcastle was evacuated to Heugh Folds for the duration of the war.

While Teresa owned the house it was said that the armchairs were kept deliberately uncomfortable to encourage good conversation after dinner! After Teresa's death in 1958 the house was acquired by her nephew Adrian Graham Merz who sold off the three Tarn Cottages in the late 1960s. In 1971 Heugh Folds was sold on the open market for the first time to a local dentist, Kenneth Makin-Taylor, and his wife Joan who are remembered in particular for the peacocks that they kept in the garden. Joan lived at Heugh Folds until 1998.

Heugh Folds was recently resold and is in the process of being renovated.

Etching from *Memoir of Anna Deborah Richardson* (1877)

54. Dunnabeck

Dunnabeck (previously known as Dunneybeck), was built in 1895 on its present site following construction of the Thirlmere aquaduct. The house is believed to have originally been constructed further down the path towards White Moss Quarries as one of the hutments occupied by the itinerant construction workers. It seems that the site engineer moved it up to its present site where it was developed into an elegant bungalow in 1895 by Casson Hodgson, a relative of the famous Levi Hodgson. The central core of the building is still the original timber, which has been slate-hung, with stone-built principal rooms either end.

The original owner was George Mercer of Liverpool, who was probably the engineer. His wife Mary Fleming, daughters and mother-in law were living there at the time of the 1901 census, but he was absent, perhaps on another construction job.

In 1907 the house was sold to Hardwicke Rawnsley (co-founder of the National Trust) then vicar of Crosthwaite who used it as his 'weekend retreat' and for family holidays.

Although on retirement in 1915, Rawnsley bought Allan Bank, he retained Dunnabeck, which on his death was left to his grand-daughter Una Hanbury. She continued to use it as a holiday home until emigrating with her daughters to America in 1940, when she reluctantly sold it.

It changed hands a couple of times in the next few years until architect Hermon Crook, bought it in 1956 from F.R.G. Chew, then headmaster of Gordonstoun School. Hermon was already living in the village at Dockwray Cottage (see **Dockwray** entry), and bought it as his 'simple mountain retreat' where he would spend many days, returning to his wife Irene at Dockwray in the evening. For a time Dunnabeck was the family's holiday home until Hermon sold it to a relative Heather Taylor, in 1968. When Charles Taylor retired in 1971, Charles and Heather moved from Bolton and enjoyed twenty-seven years at the house. Heather gifted it to the next generation of the family in 1998. It recently was sold to a family as a holiday home.

View from Dunnabeck

.

Sources and Suggested Reading

Mary L. Armitt, 'Fullers and Freeholders of the Parish of Grasmere' *Cumberland and Westmorland Antiquarian and Archaeological Society*, 1907

Mary L. Armitt, *The Church of Grasmere*, Titus Wilson, 1912

R. W. Brunskill, *Vernacular Architecture of the Lake Counties: A Field Handbook*, Faber & Faber, 1974

John F Curwen, 'Records Relating to the Barony of Kendale' Vol III, *Cumberland and Westmorland Antiquarian and Archaeological Society*, Titus Wilson, 1926

Susan Denyer and Janet Martin, *A Century in the Lake District*, National Trust, 1995

G. Elliott, 'The Decline of the Woollen Trade in Cumberland, Westmorland and Northumberland in the late 16th Century', *Cumberland and Westmorland Antiquarian and Archaeological Society*, 1960

William Farrer, 'Records Relating to the Barony of Kendale' Vols I & II, *Cumberland and Westmorland Antiquarian and Archaeological Society*, Titus Wilson, 1923/4

Clare Fell, *Early Settlement in the Lake Counties*, Dalesman Books, 1972

Robert Gambles, *Lake District Place-Names*, Dalesman Books, 1980

William Gell, *A Tour in the Lakes 1797*, ed. by William Rollinson, Smith Settle, 2000

Grasmere Women's Institute, *Golden Jubilee Scrapbook*, 1965

Grasmere Women's Institute, *Grasmere: A Short History*, ed. by Rachel MacAlpine, Kendal, 1979 [written in 1956 and published with postscript covering 1960-79]

R. A. Gregory and E. Kingston, *Reflections on History: Exploring the Industrial Archaeology of the Windermere area*, Oxford Archaeology, 2014

Grasmere Conservation Area - Appraisal and Management Plan, The Conservation Studio, Gloucester/Lake District National Park, 2008

'Grasmere, Rydal, Ambleside' in Lake District Nomination Dossier for UNESCO World Heritage Site Status, Vol. 2.13, 2015

William Heaton Cooper, *Mountain Painter: An Autobiography*, Frank Peters, 1984

C. Roy Hudleston, 'The Fleming Family: the First and Third Baronets of Rydal', *Cumberland and Westmorland Antiquarian and Archaeological Society*, 1963

Irvine Hunt, *Old Lakeland Transport*, Rusland Press, 1978

G. P. Jones, ' The Decline of the Yeomanry in the Lake Counties', *Cumberland and Westmorland Antiquarian and Archaeological Society*, 1962

John Marsh, *The Westmorland Lakes in Old Photographs*, Alan Sutton, 1992

John Marsh, *Life in Old Lakeland*, Dalesman Books, 1985

William T. Palmer, *The English Lakes*, illustr. by A Heaton Cooper, Adam & Charles Black, 1905

William Parson and William White, *A History, Directory & Gazetteer of Cumberland & Westmorland*, Leeds, 1829

Eleanor Rawnsley (née Simpson), Scrapbook, Archives of The Wordsworth Trust

J. R. Robinson et al, *Great Grandad's Army Rifle Ranges of the Lake District*, 2016

William Rollinson, *A History of Man in the Lake District*, Dent, 1967

Peter Schofield and Alastair Vannan, *Fulling Mills in Easedale, Grasmere, Elterwater, Great Langdale and Graythwaite*, Oxford Archaeology North, 2012

Peter Schofield, *Windermere Reflections, Mines and Quarries, Bank's Quarry, Greenhead Gill Mine, Fairfield Mine and Providence Mine in Grasmere and Elterwater*, Oxford Archaeology North, 2013

Gertrude M. Simpson, 'Grasmere Field Names', *Cumberland and Westmorland Antiquarian and Archaeological Society*, 1928

Ian Tyler, *Thirlmere Mines and the Drowning of The Valley*, Blue Rock, 2005

Dorothy Wordsworth, *The Grasmere Journals*, ed. by Pamela Woof, OUP, 1991

Dorothy Wordsworth, *George and Sarah Green, A Narrative*, ed. by Ernest de Selincourt, OUP, 1936

Extracts from original documents
Grasmere Millennium Collection, Wordsworth Trust

Websites
Cumbria County History Trust   www.cumbriacountyhistory.org.uk
British History Online   www.british-history.ac.uk
EdenLinks Genealogy   www.edenlinks.co.uk

Maps
Ordnance Survey Map, 1959

Contributors:

Lin Allen
Polly Atkin
David Bass
Mary Bass
Rose Barker
Christine Batey
Dennis Batey
Hilary Beskeen
Richard Beskeen
Jane Brimmer
Mary Chuck
Angela Clark
Martin Clark
Gill Cowton
Jeff Cowton
Bev Dennison
Brenda Elliott
Donald Elliott
Ann Fawthrop
Stuart Fawthrop
Adam Foster
Laurence Harwood
Melissa Harwood
Shirley Hill
Peter Hitchcock
Judy Hitchcock
Joanne Hunter

Sally Keighley
David Jackman
David Johnson
Carole Knight
Myra McCraith
Ruth Morris
Doreen Mott
Chris Norris
Jude O'Gorman
Wendy Robinson
Andrew Saalmans
Sharon Savasi
Sarah Simpson
Will Smith
Maureen Sutcliffe
Stewart Sutcliffe
Louise Sykes
Brian Taylor
Carrie Taylor
Pat Taylor
Richard Taylor
Karen Tempest
Phil Tempest
Malcolm Thorogood
Harvey Watson
Ken Wood

Special thanks to:

Rob David
Geoffrey Darrall and Patricia Darrall

The Wordsworth Trust, which has been able to support this book as part of its National Lottery Heritage Fund-assisted project, Reimagining Wordsworth.

Lightning Source UK Ltd.
Milton Keynes UK
UKHW020657070620
364513UK00003B/29